Vaccines

Vaccines

KEVIN HILLSTROM

LUCENT BOOKS

A part of Gale, Cengage Learning

GALE
CENGAGE Learning·

Detroit • New York • San Francisco • New Haven, Conn • Waterville, Maine • London

LIBRARY OF CONGRESS CATALOGING-IN-PUBLICATION DATA

Hillstrom, Kevin, 1963-
  Vaccines / by Kevin Hillstrom.
     p. cm. -- (Nutrition and health)
  Includes bibliographical references and index.
  ISBN 978-1-4205-0724-9 (hardcover)
  1. Vaccines. 2. Vaccination. I. Title.
  RA638.H55 2012
  615.3'72--dc23

                                    2012021862

Lucent Books
27500 Drake Rd.
Farmington Hills, MI 48331

ISBN-13: 978-1-4205-0724-9
ISBN-10: 1-4205-0724-9

Printed in the United States of America
1 2 3 4 5 6 7 16 15 14 13 12

TABLE OF CONTENTS

Many people today are often amazed by the amount of nutrition and health information, often contradictory, that can be found in the media. Television, newspapers, and magazines bombard readers with the latest news and recommendations. Television news programs report on recent scientific studies. The healthy living sections of newspapers and magazines offer information and advice. In addition, electronic media such as websites, blogs, and forums post daily nutrition and health news and recommendations.

This constant stream of information can be confusing. The science behind nutrition and health is constantly evolving. Current research often leads to new ideas and insights. Many times, the latest nutrition studies and health recommendations contradict previous studies or traditional health advice. When the media reports these changes without giving context or explanations, consumers become confused. In a survey by the National Health Council, for example, 68 percent of participants agreed that "when reporting medical and health news, the media often contradict themselves, so I don't know what to believe." In addition, the Food Marketing Institute reported that eight out of ten consumers thought it was likely that nutrition and health experts would have a completely different idea about what foods are healthy within five years. With so much contradictory information, people have difficulty deciding how to apply nutrition and health recommendations to their lives. Students find it difficult to find relevant, yet clear and credible information for reports.

Changing recommendations for antioxidant supplements are an example of how confusion can arise. In the 1990s antioxidants such as vitamins C and E and beta-carotene came to the public's attention. Scientists found that people who ate more antioxidant-rich foods had a lower risk of heart disease, cancer, vision loss, and other chronic conditions than those who ate lower amounts. Without waiting for more scientific study, the media and supplement companies quickly spread the word that antioxidants could help fight and prevent disease. They recommended that people take antioxidant supplements and eat fortified foods. When further scientific studies were completed, however, most did not support the initial recommendations. While naturally occurring antioxidants in fruits and vegetables may help prevent a variety of chronic diseases, little scientific evidence proved antioxidant supplements had the same effect. In fact, a study published in the November 2008 *Journal of the American Medical Association* found that supplemental vitamins A and C gave no more heart protection than a placebo. The study's results contradicted the widely publicized recommendation, leading to consumer confusion. This example highlights the importance of context for evaluating nutrition and health news. Understanding a topic's scientific background, interpreting a study's findings, and evaluating news sources are critical skills that help reduce confusion.

Lucent's Nutrition and Health series is designed to help young people sift through the mountain of confusing facts, opinions, and recommendations. Each book contains the most recent up-to date information, synthesized and written so that students can understand and think critically about nutrition and health issues. Each volume of the series provides a balanced overview of today's hot-button nutrition and health issues while presenting the latest scientific findings and a discussion of issues surrounding the topic. The series provides young people with tools for evaluating conflicting and ever-changing ideas about nutrition and health. Clear narrative peppered with personal anecdotes, fully documented primary and secondary source quotes, informative sidebars, fact boxes, and statistics are all used to help readers understand these topics and how they affect their bodies and their lives. Each volume includes information about changes in trends over time, political controversies, and international perspectives. Full-color photographs and charts enhance all volumes in the series. The Nutrition and Health series is a valuable resource for young people to understand current topics and make informed choices for themselves.

A Shield Against Sickness

Vaccination is frequently described as one of the great medical miracles of human history. When scientists learned how to make vaccines and safely deliver them to men, women, and children, they succeeded in taming numerous dreaded diseases that had disabled or killed millions of people over the centuries. The horrible small-pox virus, which claimed as many as 500 million lives in the twentieth century alone, was completely eradicated through vaccination by 1980. The nightmarish polio virus also went into full retreat in the face of immunization campaigns, and it is now on the verge of total eradication. Cases of other feared diseases, such as rubella, diphtheria, and whooping cough, have also plummeted in the United States and other medically advanced nations thanks to effective vaccination programs.

Vaccination has been so effective, in fact, that entire generations of Americans have grown up without any firsthand knowledge of the terror and heartache that some of these diseases caused. Most kids and parents in the United States now treat immunization shots as a routine part of growing up, like going to the dentist or getting your driver's license. According to the Program for Appropriate Technology in Health (PATH), a nonprofit organization that works to extend vaccination to poor people around the world, this is a remarkable accomplishment: "Only 50 years after vaccination became a standard rite of passage for children, it was taken for granted that a child born in the developed world would grow up without fear from the paralysis, brain damage, blindness and death that plagued the generations before her."[1]

In recent years, though, the wisdom of vaccination has been openly questioned, especially in the United States. Some parents and pediatricians argue that U.S. immunization programs, which now provide vaccines for fourteen different diseases, have become too burdensome and hard on kids. Other critics say that federal demands that citizens submit to vaccination constitute an attack on their personal freedoms. Meanwhile, growing numbers of parents and politicians have claimed that vaccination is a key factor in the rise in autism, attention deficit hyperactivity disorder (ADHD), and other childhood developmental disorders.

Vaccines have been so effective that entire generations of Americans have grown up without any firsthand knowledge of the terror and heartache that the diseases they have been vaccinated against can cause.

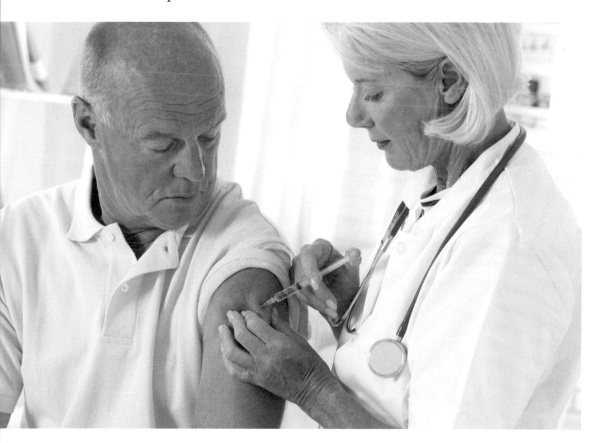

Many scientists, doctors, and policymakers have reacted to these complaints with a mixture of anger and frustration. They continue to defend vaccines as one of the greatest and most beneficial tools of modern medicine. In their view, attacks on immunization programs are based on fear and ignorance, not sound science. They also worry that as growing numbers of Americans choose *not* to vaccinate their children, the vulnerability to dangerous outbreaks of disease will grow. Their assurances, though, have failed to comfort critics. In fact, the debate over vaccination seems to grow more heated with each passing year.

CHAPTER **1**

The History of Vaccination

Over the last few centuries, the rise of vaccination has dramatically altered the history of our planet and the peoples who inhabit it. Prior to the development of vaccines, great waves of disease periodically washed over the world, claiming hundreds, thousands, and even millions of lives at a time. These severe outbreaks of disease are known today as epidemics, and they shattered families, communities, and even nations. For example, scientists now believe that the great city-state of Athens, the most famous and influential city of ancient Greece, may have been mortally weakened by an outbreak of typhoid fever around 430 B.C. The epidemic claimed so many Athenian lives—as much as one-third of the population—that the rival city-state of Sparta was able to gain the upper hand in its long and bitter conflict with Athens. This conflict, known as the Peloponnesian War, ended in a victory for the Spartans in 404 B.C.

In some cases, fearsome infectious diseases such as typhoid fever, smallpox, typhus, and bubonic plague spread so far and wide that they devastated entire continents. These continent-wide or global events are known today as pandemics. The most horrible of these pandemics was an outbreak of bubonic plague that swept across medieval Europe in the fourteenth century. Scholars believe that this outbreak, called the Black Death, may have cut Europe's entire population in half by the time it ran its course.

The world's early peoples were largely helpless in the face of these horrifying events. They vaguely understood that smallpox, bubonic plague, and other terrors could be passed from person to person. They also recognized that people who contracted a disease like smallpox and managed to survive did not have to worry about getting it again. They had no concept of germs or immune systems, however, and did not possess the scientific knowledge to protect themselves. When outbreaks of infectious disease occurred, their options were limited. All communities could do was isolate infected people—a practice known as quarantine—until they recovered. Some individuals and families, meanwhile, responded

Throughout history, epidemics have shattered families, communities, and even nations. The great plague in Athens in around 430 B.C. claimed one-third of the population.

by fleeing to more lightly populated regions, where they hoped the disease would not follow.

Many people, however, simply decided that they were at the mercy of God when disease entered their neighborhoods and homes. They comforted sick family members as best they could—then waited anxiously to see who would survive and who would perish. As scholar Arthur Allen wrote, they lived in "a world in which loved ones were swept away by diseases whose sudden appearance was as mysterious as their departure."[2]

HEALTH FACT

The face, neck, and shoulders of the mummy of Pharoah Ramses V, who died in 1157 B.C., is disfigured by a rash of elevated pustules that may have been caused by smallpox, but researchers cannot be sure of the infection that caused them.

The Smallpox Epidemic of 1721

Feelings of powerlessness toward the world's scariest infectious diseases did not begin to change until the early eighteenth century. In 1721 an influential Boston minister named Cotton Mather insisted that people actually had the capacity to protect themselves from smallpox, which at that very moment was spreading terror and death across the city. Mather had read in a British academic journal about a practice called variolation that had been utilized for centuries in some parts of Africa and Asia to combat smallpox. Under this procedure, which also came to be known as inoculation, living smallpox virus was harvested directly from sick patients. This was done by taking liquid pus from the pustules (skin sores) that typically erupted across the bodies of smallpox victims. The virus was then scratched into a healthy person's skin with a knife, needle, or other sharp instrument.

At first glance, the idea of deliberately infecting a healthy person with a deadly virus so as to protect them from that disease seemed crazy. Modern scientists know, though, that this process actually worked. These ancient African and Asian communities had figured out a way to expose healthy members to a weakened, less-dangerous version of the disease-causing virus. Only a small amount of the virus was used in variolation, and it was introduced on an arm or leg, far away from the body's vital functions. People who contracted smallpox naturally, though, typically suffered massive exposure through their respiratory systems, which also gave the disease an easy avenue to attack vital organs and other bodily systems.

Once the immune system was awakened through variolation, it would then begin generating antibodies—the chemicals that defend against dangerous germs when they enter people's bodies. Variolation could still make people sick for a few days or weeks, but the symptoms were not nearly as severe as they would be with a full-blown case of smallpox. Once the patients recovered, they had lifelong immunity from the disease.

Mather was so intrigued by the journal reports that he questioned Boston-area slaves about whether they had ever undergone variolation back in Africa. After interviewing several slaves who had been inoculated successfully, Mather became convinced that the procedure could deliver Boston from the terror of smallpox once and for all. In the spring of 1721 he called for a citywide variolation campaign against the disease. Many Boston residents were horrified by the suggestion, and most of the city's physicians denounced him. Mather did manage to persuade one doctor to take part in the experiment, however. Zabdiel Boylston began inoculating patients on June 26, 1721. He eventually completed the procedure on 248 patients.

The variolation campaign undertaken by Mather and Boylston sparked the creation of a large and vocal anti-variolation movement led by William Douglass, who was Boston's most respected physician at the time. Douglass and his allies insisted that variolation would just make the epidemic worse. In fact, they characterized Mather's campaign as a potential threat to the city's very existence. Tensions over variolation eventually became so heated that Mather's enemies firebombed his home.

As it turned out, Douglass's main charge—that variolation did not work—was wrong. Scientists agree, though, that another one of Douglass's criticisms of the Mather-Boylston inoculation campaign was valid. Douglass regularly complained that neither Mather nor Boylston required patients

who underwent variolation to be placed under quarantine. He correctly warned that this was unwise because freshly inoculated patients with smallpox in their systems had the potential to pass the disease along to unsuspecting strangers.

By the time the smallpox outbreak ran its course in early 1722, nearly 6,000 Boston residents had contracted the disease and more than 840 of them had died of it. Mather and Boylston, though, argued that the outbreak would have been even more severe had it not been for their variolation efforts. In 1726 they released a study indicating that 14 percent of Bostonians who had contracted smallpox naturally during the outbreak had died from the disease, while only 3 percent of Boylston's variolation patients had perished. Douglass and other critics initially dismissed these findings. As the 1720s unfolded, however, scientific and medical interest in variolation grew considerably. By 1730, when the next smallpox epidemic rolled into Boston, Douglass was among the city's most prominent variolators.[3]

Problems with Inoculation

During the course of the eighteenth century, physicians in the United States and Europe became increasingly supportive of smallpox inoculation. Many doctors came to feel that it was helpful in limiting the death toll from smallpox epidemics, especially if patients were carefully quarantined (usually for two weeks) after inoculation.

Physicians and public health officials took special pleasure in how inoculation changed medicine's basic approach to disease. For centuries, physicians and other health care practitioners had only treated patients *after* they fell victim to a disease. With inoculation, though, they could take action to protect patients *before* an epidemic even broke out. By mid-century, this early landmark in preventive medicine was being practiced to one degree or another in Philadelphia, Boston, New York, and other big American cities prone to smallpox outbreaks. Acceptance was also on the rise in the great cities of Europe.

Nonetheless, inoculation campaigns continued to operate under a cloud of skepticism and suspicion. Some minor smallpox outbreaks were traced to inoculated patients who had not been properly quarantined. In other cases, the lymph—the fluid drained from a smallpox pustule for use in variolation—was too old to make inoculation effective. Or it was contaminated with tetanus, syphilis, or other bacteria that could sicken or kill people who agreed to undergo inoculation.

Numerous doctors also added a bunch of unnecessary—and sometimes dangerous—preparations to the inoculation process. Even the best doctors of this era had only a limited understanding of disease and immunity. They often recommended medical treatments that were deeply flawed, and sometimes even dangerous to the patient. Other doctors were simply greedy. They ordered pre-variolation procedures so that they could pad their bills.

Pre-variolation treatments took many forms. For example, patients who were being prepared for variolation were frequently given doses of mercury, which could cause diarrhea and brain damage. Others were given a chemical called calomel, which could loosen teeth to the point that they fell out. John Adams, who later became the second president of the United States, endured both of these treatments when he was prepared for inoculation in the winter of 1764. "[My doctors] reduced me very low before they performed the operation," Adams recalled in his autobiography. "Every tooth in my head became so loose that I believe I could have pulled them all with my thumb and finger."[4]

Other popular pre-inoculation treatments included weeks of bloodletting (in which doctors would purposely cut and withdraw blood from patients to put their bodies in better "balance") and daily infusions of medicines that induced heavy vomiting. Many people were forced to endure all of these horrible treatments at the same time. Scholars believe that these preparations weakened some patients so much that they were in mortal danger of succumbing to even a weak dose of smallpox by the time the day of inoculation finally came around.

The medical profession finally moved away from these damaging preparatory treatments in the late 1700s. This change helped improve the reputation of inoculation, as did the public support of leading politicians like Thomas Jefferson and Benjamin Franklin. Another big factor was General George Washington's decision to order inoculation of the Continental Army in 1777, at the height of the Revolutionary War. This variolation campaign was so successful in reducing smallpox cases among Washington's troops that it has been credited as a factor in America's ultimately successful fight for independence from the British Empire. Historian Elizabeth Anne Fenn wrote that "Washington's unheralded and little-recognized resolution to inoculate the Continental forces must surely rank with the most important decisions of the war."[5]

By the close of the 1700s many—though not all—Americans had come around to the idea that inoculation provided both protection and peace of mind. As scholar Sarah B. Dine wrote, "Over the course of a century, inoculation had transformed smallpox from the dreaded scourge known as the 'speckled monster' to a guest encouraged to visit the family home."[6]

Edward Jenner and the Smallpox Vaccine

The next major scientific breakthrough in the battle against infectious disease came in 1796, when an English doctor named Edward Jenner performed the world's first vaccination. During the 1780s Jenner had become fascinated with a well-known phenomenon in the English countryside: milkmaids virtually never contracted smallpox, no matter how much they encountered the disease. Jenner eventually discovered that the milkmaids were immune to smallpox because they had already contracted cowpox—a related but mild disease that passed to them from the cows they tended.

In 1796 Jenner tested his hypothesis on a local eight-year-old boy named James Phipps. He took pus from a cowpox sore on a milkmaid's hand and placed it on a fresh cut in the boy's arm. Phipps became feverish and achy from the vaccination, which acquired its name from *vaccinia,* the Latin term for cowpox. He recovered in a matter of days, though, and six weeks later Jenner variolated the boy with smallpox. When the boy remained perfectly healthy, Jenner knew that he had discovered a medical treatment that would change the world.

Jenner conducted a series of other successful vaccination experiments on local farming families using lymph taken directly from infected cows. He then published his findings in a text called *An Inquiry into the Causes and Effects of the* Variolae Vaccinae (1798). Jenner's explanation of the cowpox vaccine and its power to stop smallpox took the world by storm. Within a few years the so-called Jennerian inoculation was spreading across both Europe and America. Millions of people volunteered to be vaccinated with cowpox, and Jenner became an international celebrity. "Every friend of humanity must look with pleasure on this discovery, by which one evil more is withdrawn from the condition of man,"[7] wrote Jefferson.

Jenner's cowpox vaccine was a clear improvement on the risky old technique of inoculation, which relied on immunization through exposure to actual smallpox. Vaccination had problems, too, though. One 1800 vaccination campaign in

Massachusetts had tragic results when vaccinators accidentally used smallpox rather than cowpox, killing sixty-eight people. Other vaccinations ended up providing no smallpox protection because the cowpox lymph was too old. A number of vaccines actually spread disease because they had been contaminated with syphilis or other blood-borne illnesses.

Finally, some parents, doctors, and ministers objected to the vaccine on religious grounds. Jenner's reliance on lymph from an animal led them to charge that the vaccine was a devilish violation of natural law. Some foes claimed that vaccinated children showed signs of sprouting cows' horns. An organization known as the Anti-Vaccination Society called vaccination "a gross violation of religion, law, morality, and humanity."[8] In an illustration in one 1806 book, Jenner was depicted "with a tail and hoofs, feeding basketsful of infants to a hideous monster."[9]

Compulsory Vaccination in Europe and America

As the nineteenth century unfurled, many supporters of vaccination claimed that citizens should be legally required to undergo the procedure in order to keep smallpox under control. From 1840 to 1873 Great Britain passed a series of mandatory vaccination laws despite loud objections from some of its citizens. In 1874 Germany enacted a law requiring all German children to receive smallpox vaccinations by age two, with follow-up vaccinations around age twelve.

Federal authorities in the United States were more reluctant to impose compulsory vaccination laws. A number of city and state lawmakers approved compulsory vaccination laws, however. In addition, a growing number of America's public schools made vaccination a condition of student enrollment. If a student had not been vaccinated, he or she was not welcome in the classroom. This rule was instituted in several big cities that were particularly vulnerable to epidemics.

The compulsory vaccination movement was aided by several historical developments. In both the American Civil War (1861–1865) and Europe's Franco-Prussian War (1870–1871), the eventual victors benefited greatly from their superior smallpox vaccination programs. Around this same time, the supply of high-quality smallpox vaccine soared with the creation of so-called vaccine farms. At these farms, which became popular in both the United States and Europe, large numbers of cattle were kept specifically to provide a steady flow of cowpox lymph that could be used in vaccines.

HEALTH FACT

In 1827 Boston became the first large American city to pass a compulsory vaccination law.

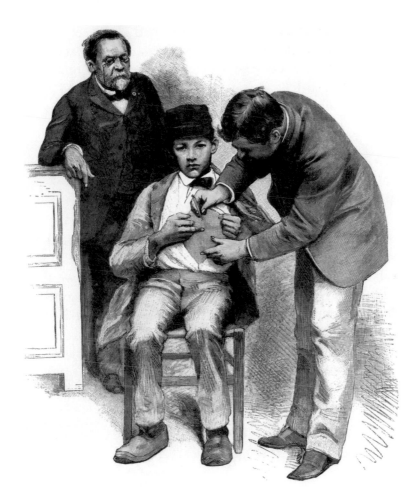

Louis Pasteur, left, supervises an inoculation for rabies. By this time, Pasteur had also developed a vaccine for chicken cholera.

Another major improvement in vaccine quality was made in the 1880s by the famed German scientist Robert Koch and his talented staff of researchers. They discovered that when cowpox lymph was stored in a chemical called glycerine, dangerous microorganisms like tetanus, syphilis, and streptococci that sometimes lurked in the vaccine were killed off. In addition, thinning the virus in glycerine enabled physicians to make the vaccine last longer and go further. As Allen wrote, "A single cow could now yield up to 6,000 vaccinations, compared with 200 to 300 doses per cow with unglycerinated vaccine."[10]

Public acceptance of vaccination also received a big boost from the famous French scientist Louis Pasteur. In the early 1880s Pasteur developed a vaccine that was effective in combating chicken cholera, which had long been a serious problem for French poultry farmers. A few years later, in 1885, Pasteur unveiled a vaccine for rabies, a relatively rare but much-feared disease that people contracted from the saliva of infected animals (usually through bites). Meanwhile, Pasteur's decision to follow Jenner's example and call his medicines "vaccines" catapulted the word into common usage. From this point forward, "vaccine" became the term used for any medicine designed to trigger immunity to a specific disease.

Other important medical breakthroughs soon came along as well. In 1888 the French biologist Émile Roux discovered the diphtheria toxin, paving the way for the development of a diphtheria antitoxin vaccine by the close of the century. Around this same time, French scientist Alexandre Yersin identified the *bacillus*, or specific form of bacteria, responsible for bubonic plague. In 1893 Russian bacteriologist Waldemar Mordecai Haffkine unveiled a primitive cholera vaccine that was somewhat effective in blunting an epidemic in India.

Vaccination in the Early Twentieth Century

Up until 1900 the United States and England had charted similar paths in terms of variolation and vaccination. They adopted fairly similar practices and policies, and the rest of the world followed their example to one degree or another. In the early decades of the twentieth century, though, the two nations parted ways in important respects.

In England, opposition among the poor and working class to compulsory vaccination became so strong that the country's political leadership backed off. In 1898 Parliament passed a law that permitted "conscientious objectors" to reject vaccination. Newspapers and vaccination opponents, meanwhile, trumpeted every horror story they could find about vaccinations that caused death. Such scare tactics resulted in a marked reduction in vaccination rates. By 1914 only half of England's population had been vaccinated for smallpox, a far cry from the 80 percent vaccination rate of 1898.

In the United States, by contrast, smallpox vaccination became mandatory in growing numbers of public schools. The ranks of cities and states that adopted compulsory vaccination laws also swelled. Public attitudes toward this trend remained mixed, though, in large part because of persistent fears about the safety of vaccines. These concerns intensified when parents heard reports like the ones that came out of Philadelphia and nearby Camden, New Jersey, in late 1901. Ninety residents of these cities—most of them children— died after receiving a vaccination for smallpox that had been unknowingly contaminated with tetanus, a deadly bacterium.

Public shock about the 1901 tetanus disaster finally convinced the U.S. Congress to take steps to make sure that American vaccines were being manufactured, shipped, and stored properly. Up to this point, reported John F. Anderson of the U.S. Public Health Service, "anyone could make a product, label it vaccine virus and place it on the market."[11] With the passage of the 1902 Biologics Control Act, federal agencies were authorized to oversee the production of vaccines. Manufacturers had to earn licenses from the U.S. Public Health Service (PHS) in order to sell vaccines and antitoxins. (Antitoxins are vaccine-type medicines that ward off diseases *after* exposure to poisonous microorganisms like diphtheria, tetanus, and botulinum.) Within a few years of the 1902 legislation, one-third of all U.S. vaccine makers had been forced to shut their doors because they could not meet the new PHS safety standards. The remaining companies were held to higher quality standards than ever before.

The move toward compulsory vaccination was also aided by the U.S. Supreme Court. In a 1905 case called *Jacobson v. Massachusetts,* the Court ruled that states had the right to insist on immunization against disease. According to the Court's reasoning, the need to protect community public health outweighed individual Americans' right to privacy.

Deadly Reminders of the Power of Contagious Diseases

During the 1910s the world received several grim reminders of the deadliness of infectious disease. A 1916 polio outbreak killed 6,000 Americans and paralyzed thousands more, most of whom were children. Typhus claimed millions of lives in Europe during World War I, which raged across that continent from 1914 to 1918. In late 1918, meanwhile, an influenza pandemic known as Spanish Flu broke out across the globe. By the time it ran its course a year later, the outbreak had claimed 675,000 American lives and taken another 20 to 40 million lives worldwide. The deadly flu "encircled the globe," in the words of Dr. Victor Vaughan, a former president of the prestigious American Medical Association (AMA). "[It] visited the remotest corners, taking toll of the most robust, sparing neither soldier nor civilian, and flaunting its red flag in the face of science."[12]

Despite such setbacks, though, the United States made continued progress in its efforts to tame the many infectious

A U.S. school gymnasium is converted into a Spanish flu ward in 1918. Spanish flu killed 675,000 Americans and 20 million to 40 million persons worldwide.

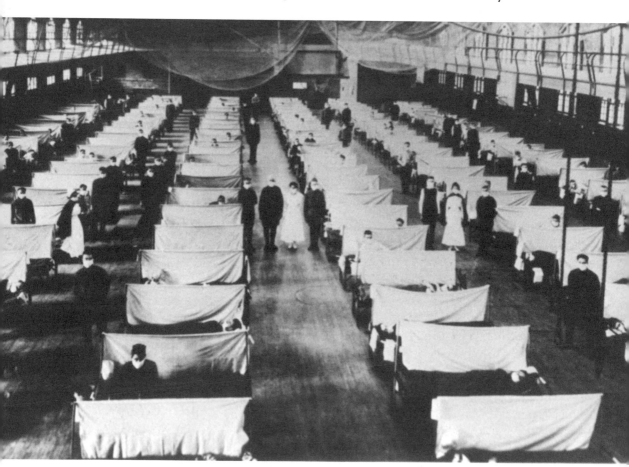

diseases that roamed the planet. In 1914 a rabies vaccine was licensed for use in the United States, and one year later vaccines for both typhoid fever and pertussis (whooping cough) became available on the U.S. market. The U.S. military also ordered mandatory typhoid vaccinations for all American troops. This precaution proved to be a wise one, for the United States suffered far fewer losses from typhoid during World War I than other armies in the conflict. Typhoid fever took only 227 American lives. The French military, by contrast, lost 12,000 soldiers to the disease in the first sixteen months of the conflict. This horrible death toll belatedly convinced French authorities to order their own mandatory vaccination program.

Vaccination's reputation benefited as well from steadily growing faith and pride in American medicine and science. "During the 1920s and 1930s scientists and physicians continued to make breathtaking gains in their ability to recognize and combat disease and other forms of sickness," explained one scholar. "These advances in medical science . . . brought about significant declines in outbreaks of infectious disease; increased reliance on both simple and complex surgical procedures; and unprecedented levels of public confidence in the drugs, therapies, and procedures that physicians prescribed for patients."[13]

Indeed, American parents gradually became more accepting of vaccination for the simple reason that it seemed to be working. Smallpox epidemics were fading in both intensity and frequency. From 1921 to 1930, for example, nearly 400,000 cases of smallpox were documented in the United States, and fewer than 1 percent of patients died. The numbers fell even more in the following decade. From 1931 to 1940 only 108,000 Americans contracted smallpox, and only 0.38 percent of them died from the disease.[14]

Vaccination campaigns had a lot to do with those numbers. Scientists have since acknowledged, however, that these impressive results were aided by the fact that a milder strain of smallpox known as *V. minor* emerged in the early twentieth century. Researchers believe that this type of smallpox, which became the dominant strain in the United States through the 1940s, may have immunized many Americans against the more lethal version, known as *V. major*.

A Healthier Generation of Americans

The introduction of new vaccines and the strengthening of existing ones greatly improved the health prospects of Americans. They were not the only factors in the improving health picture in the United States, though. During the first two decades of the twentieth century—a period known as the Progressive Era—Americans enthusiastically endorsed new laws and regulations to protect the environment and improve public health. Measures to reduce pollution in drinking water and improve the quality of the food supply made a big difference to the health of many U.S. households, especially in urban areas. In addition, America's hospitals and clinics regularly introduced new medical technologies and surgical treatments that were vast improvements over what had been available only a few decades earlier. All of these factors combined to lift average American life expectancy from forty-seven years in 1900 to sixty years in 1930.

During the post–World War I years the anti-vaccination movement faded in influence across most of the United States. Most parents raising families in cities and large towns seemed to accept that immunizing their children was a low-risk and sensible precaution. In New York City, for example, a diphtheria immunization effort vaccinated half a million children from 1929 to 1931 with little protest. Opponents of compulsory vaccination did not find a sympathetic ear in Washington, D.C., either. When one critic appeared before Congress to complain about the practice, Michigan Congressman Roy O. Woodruff responded by citing statistics indicating that typhoid, diphtheria, and other infectious diseases were not nearly the threat they once were. "How anybody having these figures before him can be opposed to vaccination and the prevention of disease is more than I can understand," Woodruff declared. "If your ideas prevailed in this country, we would still have smallpox, typhoid, and other epidemics which have now almost entirely disappeared."[15]

By the 1930s, though, public health officials warned that the great strides that America had made in combating infectious disease were giving some people too much confidence, as vaccine rates began to decline. During that decade, for example, only nine states had compulsory vaccination laws in place. "In the postwar years, rates of vaccination among the population dwindled steadily," wrote scholar James Colgrove. "Health officials often complained that physicians in private practice were lax in encouraging their patients to undergo the procedure on a routine basis. . . . Vaccination was becoming perceived as a procedure for children, which adults only rarely, if ever, needed to consider undergoing themselves."[16]

Vaccination as a Patriotic Duty

This attitude changed dramatically during and after World War II. When the United States joined Great Britain, Russia, and other nations in the battle to defeat Nazi Germany and Japan in December 1941, the U.S. government created a special wartime agency to protect American soldiers from disease. The Armed Forces Epidemiological Board oversaw huge investments of money and resources to find vaccines for tetanus, plague, meningitis, yellow fever, typhus, and other diseases.

Around this same time, scientists around the world developed insecticides like DDT, which wiped out huge numbers of malaria-carrying mosquitos and typhus-carrying lice. In fact, DDT applications were credited with virtually ending typhus in many parts of Europe (the chemical's deadly impact on bird populations and other aspects of the natural environment would not be discovered for another twenty years). Medical researchers also discovered how to mass-produce penicillin, a medicine discovered in 1928 that proved amazingly effective at fighting bacterial infections.

By the time the war ended in 1945 and American troops began streaming home to victory parades and other celebrations, appreciation for vaccines and other "miracle medicines" had reached new heights. "Vaccination had put a sanitary shield around our men, protecting them from the scourges of previous wars: typhoid fever, tetanus, smallpox, cholera, typhus, and plague," explained Allen. "Yes, the shots hurt and even caused illness sometimes, but the soldier survived. Returning from the war he wanted his children to have the same protection."[17]

After the war, in fact, many Americans came to see vaccination as an important patriotic duty. This message was driven home by people like General James Simmons, who had overseen many of the army's disease-fighting efforts during the war. "America can not fulfill her destiny as the future guardian of civilization [without good health]," he proclaimed. "A physically weak nation, like a sick man or woman, cannot hope to function successfully or to remain a leader in this barbaric world."[18]

Americans also were quick to line up for vaccinations when confronted with the threat of a genuine epidemic. When a case of smallpox was documented in New York

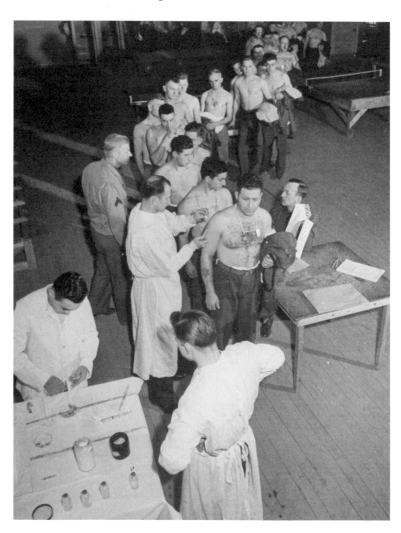

U.S. Army personnel receive vaccinations in 1942. The U.S. government created a special wartime agency to protect American soldiers from disease.

City in April 1947, for example, 6 million residents voluntarily submitted to vaccination in the space of three weeks. This prompt response strangled the outbreak before it had a chance to gain any momentum. In fact, more New Yorkers actually fell sick from the vaccine than the disease itself. America's last known outbreak of smallpox occurred two years later in Texas and was quickly contained.

The Quest for a Polio Vaccine

The 1950s and 1960s have sometimes been described as vaccination's Golden Age. During these decades scientists, lawmakers, public health officials, and drug manufacturers all worked together to advance vaccine science. They created and distributed a wide array of new vaccines to combat infectious diseases such as measles, rubella, mumps, hepatitis B (a leading cause of liver disease), and tuberculosis (which attacks the lungs). They also improved the vaccination process in other ways. By the early 1950s, for example, the United States was offering the so-called DTP vaccine—a single shot that provided protection against diphtheria, tetanus, and pertussis.

The greatest vaccination achievement of this era was the development of a vaccine against polio, a contagious virus that usually struck during childhood and caused muscle weakness, breathing problems, and paralysis. Polio had loomed as a terrifying threat to parents since ancient times, but outbreaks had steadily worsened in the opening decades of the twentieth century, killing or crippling people of every race and class.

By the 1940s, several teams of researchers across the globe were racing to see who could first develop a safe and effective vaccine against the disease, which came in three different strains, or versions. Each twist and turn in this quest was followed closely by parents in America, Europe, and around the world. "The largest medical experiment conducted in the world up to that time, it riveted the public attention like no other scientific event of the twentieth century,"[19] wrote Colgrove.

The Horrible Effects of Paralytic Polio

Back when polio constituted a major public health threat, the great majority of people contracted the disease's mildest strain, known as abortive polio. This type of polio usually only brought flu-like symptoms. The second-most common form was called nonparalytic polio, the symptoms of which included severe headache, fever, vomiting, and neck, back, and abdominal pain. The third form of polio, called paralytic polio, was the most rare—and the most feared. This strain of the disease frequently caused paralysis and death, and those who survived faced months in hospitals, breathing with the help of iron lung machines.

The doctors, nurses, and family members who tended polio sufferers described the paralytic polio wings of hospitals as places of almost overwhelming sadness. One daughter of a woman who was paralyzed with polio described the scene thusly:

In the night patients lay listening to the liquid noises of other inmates, the squish of rubber-soled nurses retreating in the corridor, and the rattle of orderlies pushing IV stands through an empty hall. When sleep eventually came, it stayed two, perhaps three hours. . . . No one could tell Mother when her pain would end; no one could control it or infuse it with meaning, or even offer an explanation for what, beyond the word polio, was causing her pain. . . . How haunting it must have been for Mother to be surrounded by the small, sober faces of suffering children, crying in the night for their own mothers.

Kathryn Black. *In the Shadow of Polio: A Personal and Social History.* Boston: Addison-Wesley, 1996, pp. 63–64.

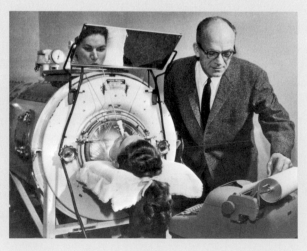

A polio victim types with her tongue as her breathing is assisted by an iron lung. Paralytic polio is a disease that frequently causes paralysis and death in children.

Salk Slays the Polio Dragon

One of the leading American polio researchers was Jonas Salk of the University of Pittsburgh School of Medicine. A brilliant virologist (virus researcher), Salk had helped develop a vaccine for two serious types of influenza during World War II. After the war he turned his attention to polio, and by 1950 he and his research team had developed a "killed-virus" vaccine treatment for all three forms of polio virus. He then carried out exhaustive trials (tests) of the vaccine with financial support from the National Foundation for Infantile Paralysis. An estimated 1.3 million U.S. children, dubbed "Polio Pioneers," took part in the final trial, which was conducted in 1954.

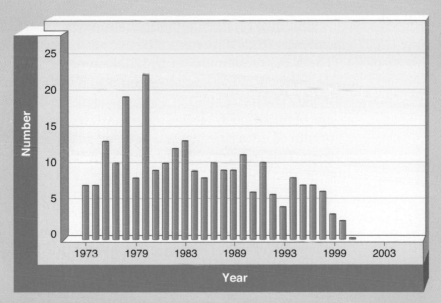

Number of Reported Cases of Polio in the United States by Year, 1973–2009

An inactivated poliomyelitis vaccine (IPV) was first licensed in 1995. An oral vaccine was licensed in 1961. No cases of vaccine-associated paralytic poliomyelitis have been reported since the IPV schedule was implemented in 2000.

Taken from: Post-Polio Health International. http://www.post-polio.org/ir-usa.html.

The Sad Origins of the Raggedy Ann Doll

The Raggedy Ann doll is one of the most famous toys in American history, but it was created under tragic circumstances. In 1915 a young girl in New York City named Marcella Gruelle received a vaccination at school without parental consent. A short time later she became paralyzed. Her father, an illustrator named Johnny Gruelle, made a rag doll featuring red yarn for hair to comfort Marcella during her illness. Marcella loved the doll, which she and her father named Raggedy Ann after a poem by James Whitcomb Riley. A short time later Marcella died. Doctors who investigated her death said that she suffered from a fatal heart defect, but her father remained convinced that the school vaccination she received had killed her.

Raggedy Ann went on to become the star of a charming series of books that Gruelle wrote and illustrated for young children. Copies of the original doll also became a fixture in the bedrooms of countless American girls. During the 1920s, though, the doll's origins and Gruelle's outspoken condemnation of vaccination also transformed Raggedy Ann into a symbol of vaccine-damaged children among anti-vaccination groups.

Arthur Allen. *Vaccine: The Controversial Story of Medicine's Greatest Lifesaver*. New York: W.W. Norton, 2007.

On April 12, 1955, authorities announced that Salk's vaccine was 80 to 90 percent effective against paralytic polio. The U.S. government immediately approved the vaccine for public use, and immunization began within a matter of weeks. The initial roll-out was marred by the discovery that one of the six polio vaccine makers, Cutter Laboratories, had produced a vaccine that was actually giving kids live polio virus. This tragedy, which became known as the Cutter Incident, resulted in the death of ten people and the permanent paralysis of two hundred others. It also sickened thousands of other inoculated children.

Once investigators figured out that the Cutter Incident stemmed from the lab's carelessness and inadequate government supervision—and not from any problem with Salk's vaccine—the national immunization campaign resumed. By the close of 1957 more than 200 million doses of his vaccine had been administered through massive immunization programs. Cases of polio fell dramatically all across the world. In the United States, for instance, the annual number of polio cases fell from more than 38,000 in 1954 to 910 by 1962.[20] By the early 2000s, polio had been completed eradicated across the United States.

In the late 1950s American researcher Albert Sabin unveiled a "live-virus" polio vaccine that eventually became more popular than Salk's creation. Sabin's version was easier to give to patients. It could be taken orally on a sugar cube, while Salk's vaccine required a shot. It also produced a quicker

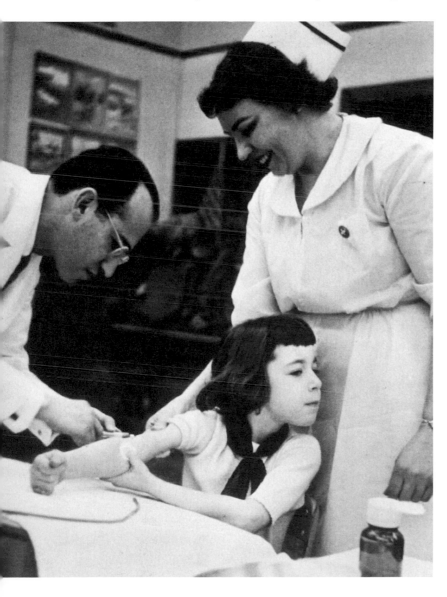

Jonas Salk inoculates a girl with the polio vaccine in 1955. Salk's polio vaccine has saved millions of lives since its introduction in the 1950s.

immune response, which meant that it was more effective in the case of a sudden outbreak of the virus.

Nonetheless, it was Salk who would always be best remembered as the scientist who first came up with an effective immunization against polio. "I was nine when the polio vaccine came out," recalled one American physician. "Dr. Salk was in the news and my parents talked about him. They were so glad, so relieved, we could get this vaccine. . . . Salk was a hero. I remember thinking this was something wonderful, to be a doctor and help people. I went into medicine because of Dr. Salk."[21]

New Controversies

In the second half of the twentieth century vaccination programs expanded all around the world. Some of the campaigns in poor countries were managed by international organizations like the World Health Organization (WHO) and the United Nations Children's Fund (UNICEF). Others were sponsored by major philanthropic organizations like the Rockefeller Foundation, Rotary International, and the Bill and Melinda Gates Foundation. Together, these efforts greatly reduced the toll of death and misery from infectious disease. Smallpox was completely eradicated around the globe. Polio vanished from American shores (the last case occurred in 1979) and was wiped out in all but a handful of other countries. As the international health organization PATH stated, whooping cough, measles, mumps, diphtheria, and other fearsome diseases were "reduced from frightening epidemics to rare outbreaks within a few decades."[22]

Beginning in the 1970s, though, vaccination also came under renewed attack in the United States. These criticisms increased in intensity and volume through the remainder of the 1900s and have remained strong in the twenty-first century. Some critics have claimed that certain vaccines have outlived their usefulness, or that they pose unnecessary health risks to children. Anti-vaccination groups have charged, for example, that vaccinations might be responsible for rising rates of autism, a disorder that severely hinders the development of social and communication skills in children.

Growing numbers of American families have responded to these concerns by rejecting immunization of their children. Prominent organizations like the American Medical Association and the American Academy of Pediatrics (AAP), which is the nation's leading organization of pediatricians, have worked mightily to reassure the public of the importance of full vaccination. Thus far, however, these educational campaigns have had only a limited impact.

CHAPTER 2

Types of Vaccines

At the most basic level, vaccination is a strategy for fooling the human body's immune system, which stands guard against dangerous bacteria, viruses, and other microorganisms that can create illness. Vaccines are designed to convince the white blood cells in the immune system that the body is under attack from one of those microorganisms. If the vaccine accomplishes this goal, white blood cells begin making antibodies. These are proteins that can destroy dangerous germs. Even after these antibodies do their work, however, they do not fade away. "They remain in the bloodstream, always on the lookout for the return of the same invaders," explains the American Academy of Pediatrics (AAP). "If these germs reappear, whether it's a few weeks or many years later, the antibodies are ready to protect. . . . That's why if you had the mumps or measles as a child, you never got it again, no matter how often you were exposed to the same infectious agent."[23]

Artificially stimulating immunity is popular because children and others who undergo vaccination gain protection from disease without having to get sick first. "This is what makes vaccines such powerful medicine," according to the Centers for Disease Control and Prevention (CDC). "Unlike most medicines, which treat or cure diseases, vaccines *prevent* them."[24]

Effective vaccines do not put any additional strain on the body's immune system, either. As the CDC explains, "A normal, healthy immune system has the ability to produce millions of these antibodies to defend against thousands of attacks every day, doing it so naturally that people are not even aware they are being attacked and defended so often."[25]

Scientists do not use just one blueprint to create these vaccines, though. Over the years they have developed vaccines using a wide range of methods and materials. Their approaches, according to the National Institute of Allergy and Infectious Diseases (NIAID), "are typically based on fundamental information about the microbe [germ], such as how it infects cells and how the immune system responds to it, as well as practical considerations, such as regions of the world where the vaccine would be used."[26] Whatever

A smallpox vaccine kit. Vaccines are designed to convince white blood cells that the body is under attack from a specific microorganism introduced by the vaccine so that the body will build a resistance to and be immune from future contact with the disease.

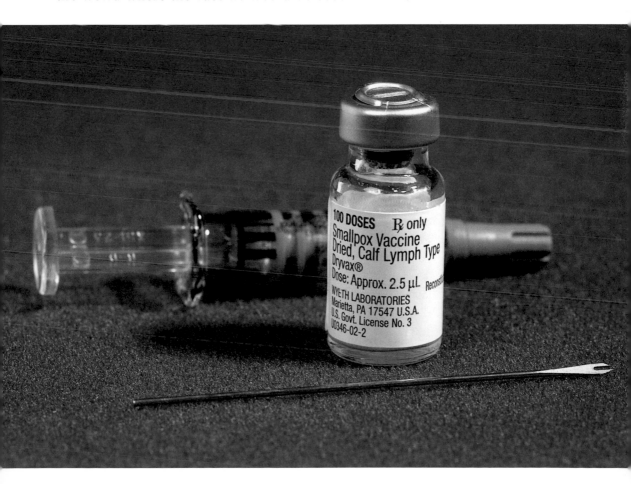

Herd Immunity

Scientists say that one of the keys to controlling infectious diseases—and perhaps even eradicating them—is to create what is known as herd immunity. The idea behind herd immunity is very simple. If an unimmunized person comes down with an infectious disease, but everyone else in the surrounding community has immunity against that disease, then the disease stays contained and does not erupt into a full-blown outbreak. With nowhere to go and no one to infect, the bacteria or virus responsible for the disease dies out.

Many American doctors and public health officials believe that herd immunity is crumbling in some parts of the country where vaccination rates are declining. As a result, outbreaks of highly contagious diseases like measles, mumps, and pertussis (whooping cough) are still popping up in some parts of the coun-

try. The Centers for Disease Control and Prevention (CDC) reported in the late 2000s, for example, that when an American boy vacationing in Europe returned to his California home, he brought measles back with him. If all of his classmates and neighbors had been immunized, herd immunity would have stopped the measles from spreading beyond that single boy. Instead, eleven of his classmates who had not received their measles shots contracted the viral disease.

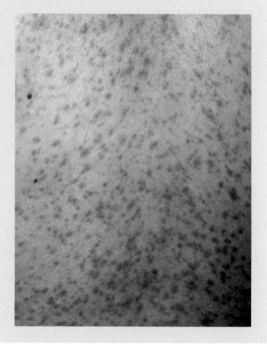

A person with measles. Many American doctors believe that herd immunity is breaking down in certain areas of the country, which is allowing outbreaks of measles, mumps, and whooping cough—all highly infectious diseases.

the circumstances, though, each vaccine has been painstakingly crafted to trigger the creation of antibodies that can provide immunized people with lasting protection against specific diseases. In many cases, this protection can last a lifetime. Other antibodies created by vaccines, though, fade in strength over time. That is why additional vaccinations, known as booster shots or booster doses, are recommended for some infectious diseases.

"Live" and "Killed" Vaccines

Vaccines have historically been divided into live vaccines and killed or inactive vaccines. Live vaccines contain weakened pathogens that have been modified so that they give immunized people enough exposure to generate immunity without triggering the actual onset of the disease. These pathogens are weakened—or "attenuated," in the terminology of scientists—through genetic engineering or exposure to animal tissues. Another way of thinking of live vaccines is that they are heavily diluted versions of the real disease.

The primary advantages of live vaccines is that they are relatively easy to produce and can often provide lifelong immunity. "Because a live, attenuated vaccine is the closest thing to a natural infection," explains the NIAID, "these vaccines are good 'teachers' of the immune system."[27] Live vaccines do mutate into potentially dangerous forms on rare occasions, though, and they are often not an option for people with weakened immune systems, such as people who have undergone chemotherapy for cancer. Live vaccines also need to be refrigerated, which makes them tough to use in developing countries with limited access to refrigeration.

Killed vaccines, by contrast, contain pathogens that have been killed by exposure to heat, radiation, or various chemicals. For many years formaldehyde was the chemical of choice for this procedure, but in recent years scientists have turned to a chemical called betapropiolactone. These types of vaccines are not as effective as live vaccines, but they do not require refrigeration so they are frequently used overseas in developing countries.

Within the killed and live categories, scientists have created vaccines to treat both bacteria- and virus-based infectious diseases. Thus, there are four main classifications of vaccines: live-virus vaccines, live-bacteria vaccines, killed-virus vaccines, and killed-bacteria vaccines.

The best-known live-virus vaccines include the ones that scientists have developed over the years against measles, mumps, rotavirus, rubella, and smallpox. Albert Sabin's oral polio vaccine is one of the most famous examples of a live-virus vaccine.

Among live-bacteria vaccines, the most prominent example has long been the Bacille Calmette-Guerin or BCG vaccine. This medicine has remained the world's only proven vaccine against tuberculosis since its introduction in 1921. The World Health Organization estimates, in fact, that more than 1 billion people have been vaccinated against tuberculosis with BCG. In recent years, however, scientists involved in the field of genetic engineering have devoted a lot of time to investigating possible new vaccines that could be created using genetically modified live bacteria.

The most famous killed-virus vaccine was the one developed by Jonas Salk in the 1950s to deliver immunity against polio. These types of vaccines were common in the early

This electron micrograph shows the vaccinia virus used in the smallpox vaccine.

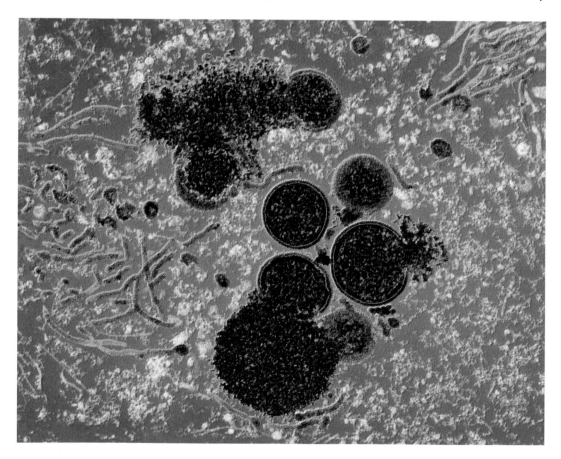

decades of vaccination, but in many cases they have been replaced by live-virus versions that are regarded as more effective in providing lifetime immunity against most diseases.

Examples of killed-bacteria vaccines include the first vaccines that were developed to combat pertussis (whooping cough), cholera, and typhoid fever. These vaccines were once regarded as marvels of modern medicine, and their arrival reined in diseases that had terrorized nations for thousands of years. Today, however, they have mostly been phased out in favor of a new class of vaccine known as bacterial subunit vaccines.

New Innovations in Vaccine Creation

Bacterial subunit vaccines are composed of specially selected antigens—substances that trigger an immune response. With this approach, scientists use only the parts of the microbe that trigger the strongest reaction from our immune system. According to the NIAID, "identifying which antigens best stimulate the immune system is a tricky, time-consuming process."[28] Once they do so, though, scientists are able to create vaccines featuring a potent blend of twenty or more antigens.

Special kinds of subunit vaccines called recombinant subunit vaccines are also being created through the science of genetic engineering to combat diseases such as hepatitis B. The process of making these vaccines begins when a scientist inserts a gene that has been coded for a vaccine protein into either 1) another "carrier" virus or 2) cells that are being grown in a laboratory. When the carrier virus reproduces or when the cell metabolizes the protein, a new vaccine protein is created.

Conjugate vaccines are similar to recombinant vaccines in that they are made when scientists mix two different components together. Conjugate vaccines, though, are made by combining the outer coating of bacteria with a carrier protein. These complex vaccines are frequently used for infants and small children with immature immune systems. The best-known vaccine that has been made using this technology is the one for *Haemophilus influenza* type b, also known as Hib disease. This disease was once the leading cause of bacterial meningitis in the United States for kids under five years of age. Meningitis is a devastating infection of the spinal cord and brain that can lead to brain damage, deafness, and other serious health problems. Prior to the development of the Hib vaccine, about twenty thousand children contracted the disease every year. By 2008 this number had dropped to thirty.

Yet another type of vaccine is the toxoid vaccine. Some bacterial diseases (such as tetanus and diphtheria) are not caused by bacteria themselves, but by the harmful chemicals—known as toxins—that those bacteria produce. Scientists took note of this important distinction, and they have figured out how to produce vaccines that neutralize these toxins. In essence, they create harmless "toxoid" versions of the dangerous toxin that trigger an immune system response. Once the immune system has created antibodies to defend against the toxoid material, those antibodies will also block the toxin if it appears. "Toxoids can actually be considered killed or inactivated vaccines," notes the History of Vaccines website, which is a project of the College of Physicians of Philadelphia. "But [they] are sometimes given their own category to highlight the fact that they contain an inactivated toxin, and not an inactivated form of bacteria."[29]

Scientists are also exploring DNA vaccines, though they remain largely experimental at this point. Researchers are very excited about this immunization technology, which is based on the idea of injecting patients with DNA coding for a particular antigen. The DNA would then insert itself into the patient's cells, which would respond by producing antigens themselves. Since the antigen is foreign, it would generate an effective immune response. According to the NIAID, scientists believe that they may one day be able to turn the body's own cells into "vaccine-making factories, creating the antigens necessary to stimulate the immune system."[30]

HEALTH FACT

According to the Centers for Disease Control and Prevention, only half of America's teenagers have received the meningococcal vaccine, which protects against bacterial infections that can lead to amputation of infected limbs (and even death in some cases).

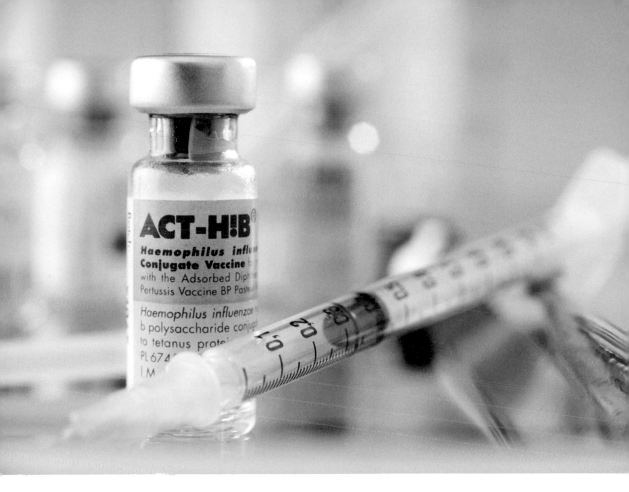

Vaccine researchers hope that one or more of these new technologies will allow them to unlock effective forms of immunization for illnesses that continue to threaten humankind. These diseases include malaria, tuberculosis, and AIDS (Acquired Immune Deficiency Syndrome).

New Vaccine Delivery Techniques

Most of the publicity surrounding vaccination research centers on efforts to develop new or improved vaccines for the people who need them. This focus is understandable, but researchers are also devoting a lot of time and effort to find new and improved ways to *deliver* existing and future vaccines to people.

One immunization method that has increased in popularity is vaccination in a nasal spray rather than injection.

The best-known conjugate vaccine is the one for Hib disease, the leading cause of bacterial meningitis in U.S. children under the age of five.

Vaccinating Endangered Species

Vaccinating against disease is usually associated with humans. Scientists and conservationists, however, have also used immunization to help endangered species of animals survive. Diseases stalk the animal kingdom just as they do the world of humans, and animals that are facing extinction from overhunting, loss of habitat, pollution, and other factors are at special risk from these viruses and bacteria.

With this in mind, some special programs have been established by governments and environmental organizations to shield already threatened species from disease outbreaks. In 2004, for example, British scientists carried out an effective rabies vaccination campaign on endangered Ethiopian wolves to limit the impact of an outbreak. One year later, Kenya carried out a successful anthrax vaccination program to protect the nation's endangered population of Grevy's zebras. Similar programs are being considered for a variety of other endangered species, including gorillas threatened by Ebola virus. "The vaccination of wildlife, when appropriate and strategically used, is a safe, direct and effective method of reducing extinction threats," said Dr. Karen Laurenson in an interview with the Reuters news agency.

Quoted in Patricia Reaney. "Targeted Vaccination Could Save Endangered Species." Reuters. On Environmental News Network, October 12, 2006. www.enn.com/top_stories/article/5236.

Snow leopards look out of their enclosure after being vaccinated. Vaccinating the endangered big cat is part of a snow leopard breeding program.

Nasal sprays, for example, have been created that are effective in vaccinating against influenza. This area of research has been praised by pediatricians and parents who say that vaccinating children would be a much easier if they did not have to subject kids to so many shots. Many children get extremely anxious and worried prior to getting shots, so vaccine nasal sprays would likely keep kids calmer and more relaxed during the immunization process.

Similarly, research has been undertaken to deliver flu immunizations through patches applied on the arm. Unlike shots by syringe, which usually have to be delivered by a trained medical person for safety reasons, both patch and nasal applications could be applied by parents or other people without any training. Supporters of this research say that either method of immunization would make it easier to vaccinate people in remote regions or undeveloped countries,

A twelve-year-old boy is vaccinated with an intranasal vaccine for swine flu. Nasal sprays and patch vaccinations are relatively new vaccine delivery systems.

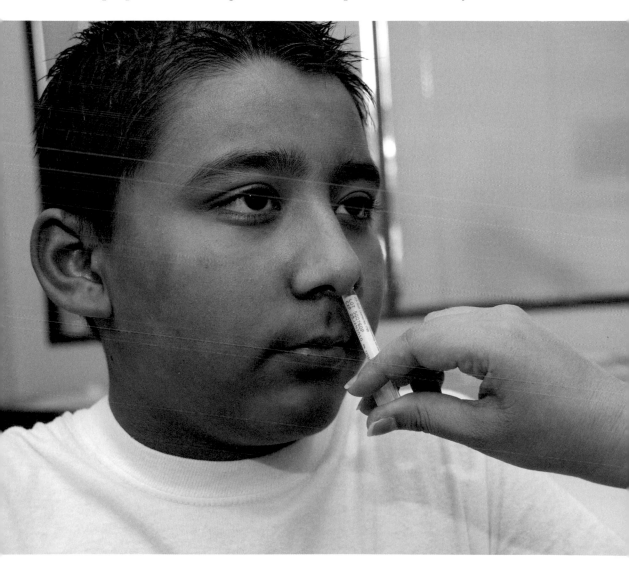

where trained doctors, nurses, and other medical personnel are rare.

Finally, researchers point out that many of the world's worst contagious diseases are now concentrated in developing countries in tropical or desert climates. This situation has led scientists to devote growing attention to developing vaccines that do not require storage in cold temperatures. In the meantime, some international health organizations have tried to overcome this obstacle by funding the acquisition of refrigerated storage units for hospitals, trucks, cargo planes, and other transport vehicles in these parts of the world.

Troubles in the Vaccine-Making Business

Although researchers and doctors are very excited about some of the new vaccine-making and vaccine-delivery technologies, they also warn that such innovations will not make any difference if drug makers are not willing to invest in them. From 1955 to 2010 the number of vaccine-making pharmaceutical companies in the United States dropped from twenty-seven to five. Today, many of the country's main childhood vaccines, including the chickenpox and measles/mumps/rubella (MMR) vaccines, are produced by just one company.

Most of the drug makers who left the vaccine business did so for the same reason: money. Clinical tests to ensure the safety of vaccines became more and more expensive. Lawsuits against vaccine makers by people who claimed injury from their products also became more common. Even in cases where the drug companies won these court cases, they sometimes incurred hundreds of millions of dollars in legal expenses.

The biggest factor in the decline in interest in vaccine-making, though, is that most vaccines just do not generate enough profit. "Vaccines are not traditionally big money makers," acknowledges Dr. Paul Offit, a prominent pediatrician and vocal defender of vaccination. "They're given once or a few times in one's life, so they're never going to be blockbusters."[31] Offit notes, though, that a few new vaccines have become sufficiently profitable to keep some drug companies in the vaccination-making business. One such drug is Prevnar, a vaccine that protects against *Streptococcus pneumoniae,* a bacteria that can cause pneumonia, meningitis, ear infections, arthritis, and other health problems. Another profitable drug that has come along in recent years is Gardasil®, which provides immunization against certain cancers caused by the human papillomavirus (HPV).

CHAPTER 3

Waging War Against Disease

Thanks in large part to vaccines, people in the United States, Canada, Europe, and other developed parts of the world are safer from most infectious diseases now than they ever have been before. Smallpox has been eradicated around the world, and infectious diseases like polio have not been seen on American soil in decades. Rates of infectious disease are also falling in many developing countries.

These trends are a cause for celebration among doctors, scientists, public health officials, and parents around the world. They do not mean, however, that the risk of contracting other diseases has completely disappeared. Authorities say that children and adults who remain unvaccinated or fail to get booster shots are still vulnerable to a wide range of infectious diseases. Infants who are not yet old enough to receive their immunization shots can still be struck down by diseases as well. In addition, some vaccines—like the one for measles—are not yet 100 percent effective in warding off disease.

Some diseases, in fact, are making comebacks. For example, annual cases of pertussis (whooping cough) have risen steadily from 1990 to 2010 in the United States. Researchers believe that this increase is related in large part to growing numbers of people who have never been vaccinated against the disease or have failed to get their pertussis booster shots. Another factor is the increased popularity of new whooping cough vaccines that have milder side effects than the old vaccines but that also do not provide the same level of immunity. Physicians and public health experts point to the tragic stories of children like Gabrielle Romaguera to emphasize that the war against pertussis and other contagious diseases has not yet been won.

Annual cases of pertussis, or whooping cough, have risen steadily from 1990 through 2010 in the United States because of a growing number of people who do not get vaccinated for it.

Gabrielle, or Brie as she was called by her family, was a happy and healthy baby during her first weeks of life. Just before turning one month old, though, Brie began coughing. Her parents, who lived in New Orleans, promptly took her to their pediatrician for a check-up. Both the pediatrician and the local hospital diagnosed Brie with a bad cold. This is a common mistake when it comes to pertussis, because the early symptoms of the disease are very similar to those that people experience when they are dealing with a cold, the flu, or bronchitis.

Brie's coughing fits worsened over the next few days, to the point that she was having trouble breathing. Her alarmed parents took her back to the hospital per the pediatrician's instructions, whereupon Brie's coughing became so bad that she passed out.

Brie was quickly transported by helicopter to a bigger hospital, where more advanced treatment was available. Unfortunately, doctors still did not realize that she was suffering from pertussis, also known as whooping cough. By the time the hospital figured out that she had a pertussis infection, Brie's life was in grave danger. The doctors treating her took a series of steps to try to save her, but these increasingly desperate efforts fell short. The infection had caused so much bleeding in her brain that little Brie could not be saved. She died on March 6, 2003—seven days before she was scheduled to receive her first immunization shot for pertussis.[32]

Infectious Disease Trends in America and Around the World

According to organizations like the Centers for Disease Control and Prevention (CDC), reported cases of most vaccine-preventable diseases have reached historic lows in the United States. A few vaccine-preventable diseases are bucking this trend, though, and some infectious diseases that have been mostly stamped out in America remain a dire threat in other parts of the world.

Before a vaccine became available, virtually every kid in the United States got chicken pox (varicella). This was usually not a big deal, since symptoms in most cases did not amount to more than a fever and an extremely itchy rash. In some serious cases, though, it could also cause skin infections and a condition called encephalitis, in which the brain swells dangerously. Since the 1995 introduction of the chicken pox vaccine in the United States, the annual number

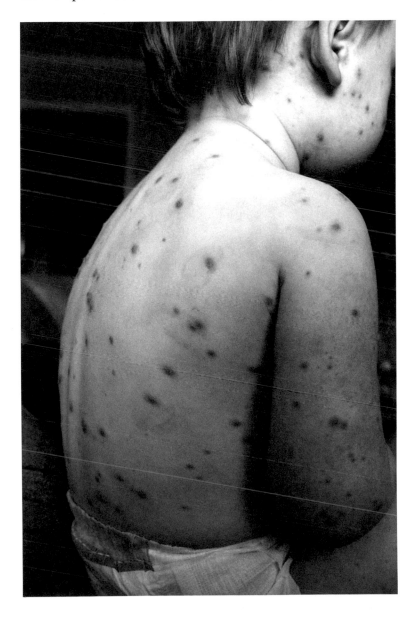

A bad case of chicken pox is seen here. Since the introduction of a chicken pox vaccine in 1995, the annual number of chicken pox cases has dropped from 4 million cases to approximately 400,000 today.

of chicken pox cases has dropped from about 4 million in the pre-vaccine era to 400,000 or so today. Chicken pox remains common in other parts of the world, especially in regions with a tropical climate.

Diphtheria is a bacterial infection that attacks the respiratory tract. It was once a deadly threat to American children.

Diphtheria and Guinea Pigs

In the late nineteenth century, scientists seeking a vaccine for the dreaded disease diphtheria frequently used guinea pigs to test their medicines. The little rodents, which originated in the mountains of South America, were regarded as ideal test subjects. They were easy to handle and transport. Even more importantly, they were very susceptible to diphtheria, unlike rats, mice, and other rodents that were sometimes used in laboratories.

The decision to inject guinea pigs with diphtheria virus, though, was controversial in some parts of Europe. Some people argued that it was immoral to sacrifice these little animals to science. They also claimed that experiments with guinea pigs did nothing to prove that medicines would be safe for human use. These critics strongly objected when scientists began extending their diphtheria vaccination experiments to human subjects.

Famed Irish playwright George Bernard Shaw accused scientists of seeing a vaccinated child in the same way that they saw guinea pigs, as "something to experiment on with a view to arranging the world." Shaw's comments were so widely distributed that "guinea pig" entered the English language as a term used to describe anyone or anything being used for morally questionable experimentation or testing.

Quoted in Arthur Allen. *Vaccine: The Controversial Story of Medicine's Greatest Lifesaver.* New York: W.W. Norton, 2007, p. 124.

Since the late nineteenth century, guinea pigs have been used to test new vaccines.

Back in the 1920s, in fact, diphtheria outbreaks infected an estimated 100,000 to 200,000 people per year, and annual deaths from the disease sometimes exceeded 15,000. Vaccination programs have played a vital role in beating back this disease over the years, though, and cases of diphtheria in the United States are now very rare. From 2000 to 2007, for example, only 3 cases were reported to the CDC. It remains a serious problem in other parts of the world, however. In 2012 the CDC reported that diphtheria was endemic (present) in nearly sixty countries.

Hepatitis A is a virus that can cause serious and even fatal liver disease. It is usually spread through contact with fecal matter. According to the CDC, there were nearly 57,000 reported cases of Hepatitis A in the United States in 1970 (a rate of about 28 cases per 100,000 people). Twenty years later, the CDC reported nearly 31,500 cases (about 12.6 cases per 100,000 people). Since a vaccine for this virus became available in the United States in 1995, however, rates have plummeted. In 2009 there were fewer than 2,000 cases of Hepatitis A in America—about 0.6 cases per 100,000 people.

Hepatitis B also causes liver damage, but this virus spreads through contact with blood and other bodily fluids. Some people never completely recover from this disease, and about 3,000 to 5,000 of these chronically infected individuals died each year in the pre vaccine era. America began vaccinating children against the virus in 1991, and rates have declined by 82 percent since 1990. It still poses a significant public health problem, however. The CDC estimated that the United States experienced 43,000 new Hepatitis B virus infections in 2007 alone. The Hepatitis B problem is much worse in other parts of the world. According to the World Health Organization (WHO), about 2 billion people worldwide have been infected with the virus, and about 350 million live with chronic infection. WHO estimates that 600,000 people die each year from health problems related to hepatitis B.

Haemophilus influenzae type b (Hib) is a virus that can cause meningitis (an infection that attacks the covering of the brain and spinal cord), pneumonia, epiglottitis (a severe throat infection), and other dangerous health problems. Before the so-called Hib vaccine was introduced for use in

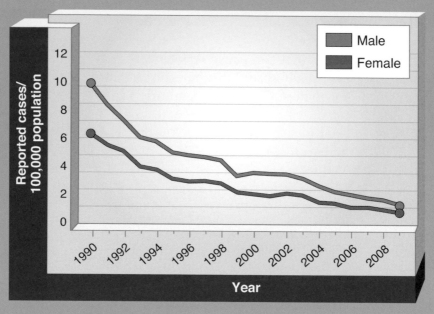

Incidence of Acute Hepatitis B, by Sex in the United States, 1990–2009

Incidence of Hepatitis B in the United States among both men and women fell dramatically after vaccination began in 1991.

Taken from: National Notifiable Disease Surveillance System. http://www.cdc.gov/hepatitis/Statistics/2009 Surveillance/Slide3.3.htm.

the United States in 1997, this virus caused about 20,000 cases of serious disease every year across America. The disease has become much less common since then. In 2008 about 2,500 cases of Hib were reported to the CDC.

Worldwide, WHO estimated that Hib caused at least 8.13 million cases of serious disease in 2000—and around 370,000 deaths of young children. Since that time, the virus has been brought under control in many wealthy, industrialized countries, where the Hib vaccine has been added to standard immunization schedules. In other nations, however, vaccination against Hib continues to lag. In China and

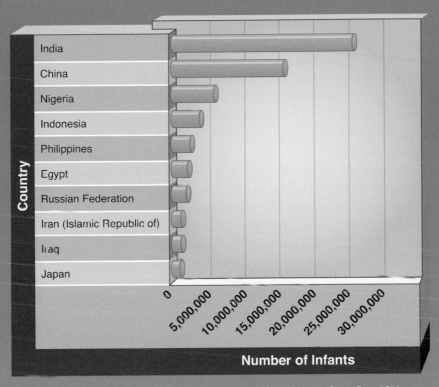

Top 10 Countries with Highest Number of Infants Not Vaccinated with 3 Doses of Hib Vaccine, 2010

Country: India, China, Nigeria, Indonesia, Philippines, Egypt, Russian Federation, Iran (Islamic Republic of), Iraq, Japan

Number of Infants: 0, 5,000,000, 10,000,000, 15,000,000, 20,000,000, 25,000,000, 30,000,000

Taken from: WHO/UNICEF coverage estimates 1980-2010, July 2011, 193 WHO Member States. Date of Slide: September 26th, 2011. http://www.who.int/nuvi/hib/decision_implementation/en/index1.html.

India, which rank as the world's two most heavily populated countries, millions of children are still not vaccinated against this highly infectious disease.

Measles is a highly contagious disease that can cause deafness, blindness, encephalitis, and death. In the 1960s the first commercial vaccine to immunize against measles became available, and since that time vaccines against other strains of measles have been developed. Between 2000 and 2007, measles deaths dropped by 74 percent worldwide. It has been almost completely eradicated in the United States and other wealthy industrialized nations. In America, for example, only 222 cases of measles were reported in 2011, most of which were traced to overseas vacations. However, about 18 to 20 million people around the world still come down with measles annually, and the disease still claims the lives of 200,000–500,000 people every year. Children in India account for about half of these deaths.

Mumps is regarded as one of the milder infectious diseases that can hit children, but it can still lead to serious health problems like meningitis, encephalitis, or deafness in rare cases. Mumps occurs worldwide, but it is fairly rare in the United States. Vaccination against mumps in the United States began in the mid-1960s, and its effectiveness in combating the disease quickly became evident. In 1970, for instance, more than 104,000 cases of mumps were reported in the United States. By 2008 the number of U.S. mumps cases had dropped to less than 500. Occasional larger outbreaks of mumps do still occur in America, however. In 2009–2010, for example, a mumps outbreak in the northeastern United States infected more than 3,500 people.

This girl's face shows the swelling of glands in the throat due to infection with the mumps virus. Mumps can lead to more serious health problems such as meningitis, encephalitis, and deafness.

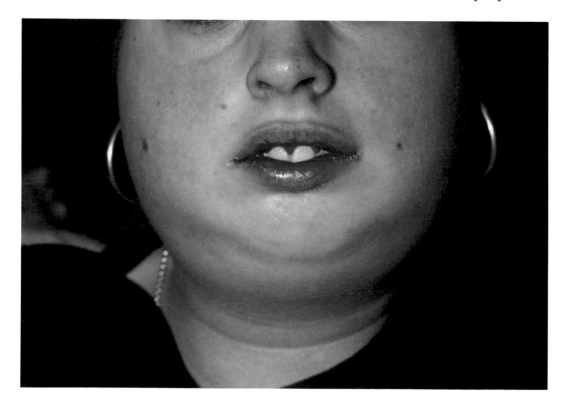

Pertussis (whooping cough) remains a feared childhood disease around the world. It is highly contagious (even people who are fully immunized can sometimes catch it), and its symptoms can be life-threatening for children. Cases of whooping cough can result in pneumonia, seizures, and brain infections. WHO reported about 16 million cases of pertussis worldwide in 2008, with approximately 195,000 deaths. The overwhelming majority of these cases (95 percent) occurred in developing countries.

Whooping cough is less of a threat in the United States, but flare-ups of the disease do occur on a regular basis. Scientists also report that pertussis rates are rising in the United States due to declining rates of vaccination. In 2000, for example, the CDC reported 7,867 cases of pertussis in America. Ten years later, 27,550 cases of pertussis were reported to the CDC (for both 2000 and 2010, the CDC believes that the actual number of cases was higher than reported). The CDC also reported a pertussis death toll of twenty-seven Americans in 2010, twenty-five of whom died before reaching their first birthday.

Pneumococcal disease is caused by different strains of bacteria that attack various parts of the body. Pneumococcal pneumonia attacks the lungs, for example, while pneumococcus bacteria can also cause meningitis, which attacks the membranes around the brain and spinal cord. Another common form of pneumococcal disease causes a condition called bacteremia, which is an infection of the blood. The CDC estimates that pneumococcal disease causes about 4,800 deaths annually across the United States. The National Foundation for Infectious Disease also reports that there are an estimated 175,000 hospitalized cases of pneumococcal pneumonia, 34,500 cases of bacteremia, and 2,200 cases of meningitis each year in the United States. Different vaccines are available for elderly people and infants, but public health authorities say that about one-third of Americans over the age of sixty-five have never been vaccinated against this disease.

Poliomyelitis (better known as polio) was one of the most feared infectious diseases in America during the first half of the twentieth century. Vaccination campaigns stamped it out in the United States, though, and scientists hope to

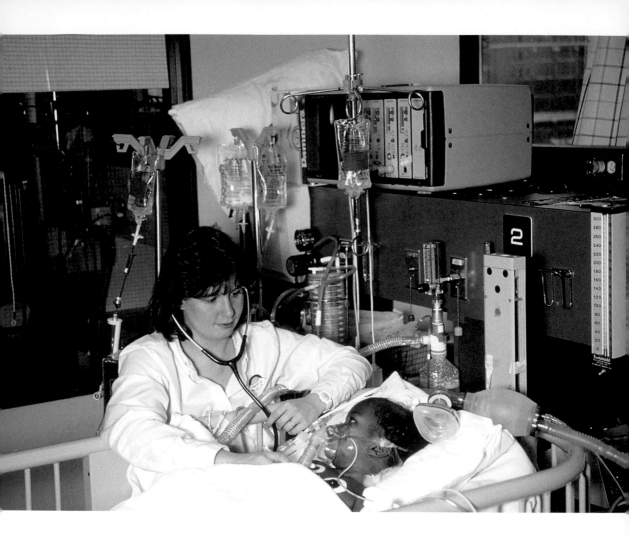

A nurse tends to a child with severe meningitis, an inflammation of the meninges, the membranes that protect the brain and spinal cord. About twenty-two hundred meningitis cases are reported each year in the United States.

push polio to extinction all around the world, just as they did smallpox. "Mass immunization campaigns which reach hundreds of millions of children in a few days have had a dramatic impact on the disease," reported the World Health Organization. "Children have been reached in some of the remotest corners of the world. Health workers have used camels, horses, dug-out canoes, boats and motor-bikes to get the vaccines through. In many countries polio immunization campaigns have been used to deliver vitamin A supplements as well, increasing the impact of immunization on child health."[33]

Today, experts agree that these mass immunization efforts have pushed polio to the brink of extinction. In 2010 the

WHO's Global Polio Eradication Initiative found only 1,352 cases of polio worldwide. The organization also reported that for the first time in its history, India—the second-most populous nation in the world—did not record a single case of polio for a one-year period (from early 2011 to early 2012). This announcement was all the more remarkable considering that as recently as 2009, India had more cases of polio (741) than any other nation in the world.

One Family's Battle with Pneumococcal Disease

In 2000 infant twins Peter and Andy received PCV7, a pneumococcal vaccine that protects against seven common types of pneumococcal bacteria. Three years later, though, the boys were infected with another type of pneumococcal bacteria that was not in the PCV7 vaccine. Their parents rushed them to the hospital, where doctors eventually realized that they were being attacked by a strain of pneumococcal disease.

Over the next few days both boys developed pneumonia and empyema, which is a severe lung complication of pneumonia. Andy also was diagnosed with hemolytic uremic syndrome, which can cause kidney failure. Doctors responded by placing tubes in the chests of both boys to drain fluid from around their lungs. Peter reacted well to this treatment, but Andy's infection worsened. He was placed in the intensive care unit and put on life support. "Seeing Andy on life support and dialysis to help his kidneys function was our worst nightmare," recalled his mother, Andrea. "We weren't sure if he was going to make it."

After four days Andy's condition improved enough for him to be taken off life support. About three weeks later the twins were able to go home, but it still took a long time for them to fully recover. "Andy was so sick and didn't talk for so long," said Andrea. "Peter needed physical therapy to help him walk." Eventually, however, both twins made a full recovery. "I feel so lucky that my boys are still here with us today," said Andrea. "I encourage every parent to get the pneumococcal vaccine for their children."

The Centers for Disease Control and Prevention supports Andrea's message. The agency also emphasizes that pneumococcal vaccine now protects against thirteen types of pneumococcal bacteria, including the type that infected Peter and Andy back in 2003. In recognition of the wide range of protection it provides, it is known as PCV13.

Centers for Disease Control and Prevention. "So Many Treatments," May 2011. www.cdc.gov/vaccines/vpd-vac/pneumo/unprotected-story.htm.

Rotavirus infections can trigger severe bouts of vomiting and diarrhea in small children. Prior to the development of a vaccine, this highly contagious virus accounted for the hospitalization of 50,000 to 70,000 children annually (and about 20 to 60 deaths) in the United States. Two rotavirus vaccines were developed and approved for use in the United States in 2006 and 2008, and these medicines have already begun to reduce rotavirus infections in America.

Immunization programs for rotavirus are also being implemented in developing countries, where the disease is far more common. Rotavirus is transmitted via fecal matter, which often gets into the water or food supply of countries with poor sanitation infrastructure. According to the private immunization group PATH, rotavirus

A young Indian girl receives polio vaccine through the Global Polio Eradication Initiative of the World Health Organization (WHO). In 2010 the WHO reported only 1,352 polio cases worldwide.

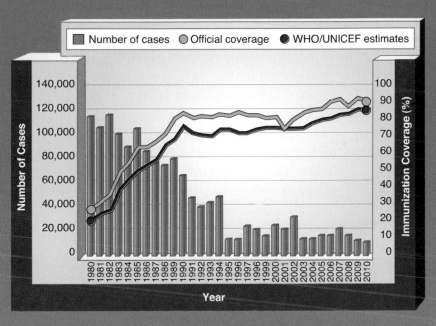

Total Reported Tetanus Cases Worldwide and Tetanus Vaccine Coverage, 1980–2010

Number of cases ▮ Official coverage ○ WHO/UNICEF estimates ●

Number of Cases — 140,000, 120,000, 100,000, 80,000, 60,000, 40,000, 20,000, 0

Immunization Coverage (%) — 100, 90, 80, 70, 60, 50, 40, 30, 20, 10, 0

Year — 1980, 1981, 1982, 1983, 1984, 1985, 1986, 1987, 1988, 1989, 1990, 1991, 1992, 1993, 1994, 1995, 1996, 1997, 1998, 1999, 2000, 2001, 2002, 2003, 2004, 2005, 2006, 2007, 2008, 2009, 2010

Taken from: World Health Organization. www.who.int/immunization_monitoring/diseases/tetanus/en/index.html.

accounts for 2 million hospitalizations and the deaths of 500,000 children from diarrheal disease each year in the developing world.

Rubella (German measles) only causes mild rash and fever symptoms in most cases, but it poses a grave danger to pregnant women and their unborn children. "If a woman gets rubella early in her pregnancy," reports the CDC, "there is an 80 percent chance her baby will be born deaf or blind, with a damaged heart or small brain, or mentally impaired."[34] This condition is known as Congenital Rubella Syndrome (CRS).

After being introduced in 1969, the rubella vaccine greatly reduced the toll of this disease. In America, for example, the number of cases of rubella declined from more than 56,500 in 1970 to fewer than 4,000 in 1980—and only 16 by

2008. Worldwide, however, about 110,000 people are still infected with rubella each year.

Tetanus, commonly called lockjaw, is unlike most other infectious diseases in that it does not pass from person to person. It is contracted through a cut or wound that becomes contaminated with tetanus bacteria, which can be found in soil, dust, and manure. The bacteria then attack the nervous system, where they can cause such severe muscle spasms that the infected person's jaw becomes "locked." The condition makes it difficult to open the mouth or swallow. In the worst cases, it can even lead to death from suffocation. Tetanus is very rare in the United States, thanks to a well-established immunization program that includes booster shots every ten years. The United States averages only about 50 cases of tetanus annually. Worldwide, WHO reported 9,683 tetanus cases in 2010. This figure marks a better than 90 percent decline in tetanus since the early 1980s, when global tetanus vaccination programs were introduced.

The tetanus bacterium, Clostridium tetani, *is shown. A 90 percent decline in tetanus cases has been seen since global tetanus vaccinations were started in the 1980s.*

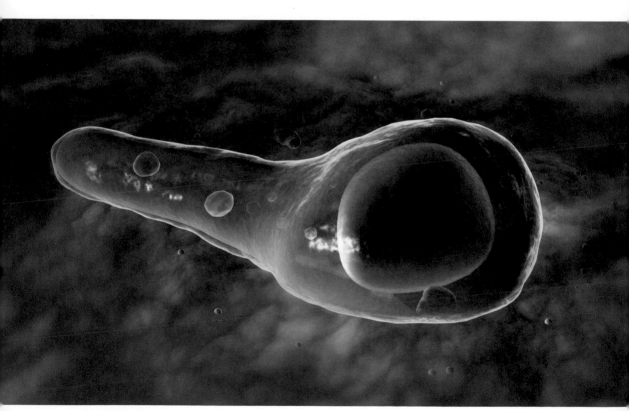

Some Battles Won, Others Still Being Waged

Scientists who have examined historical trends of various infectious diseases speak with a single voice about the importance of vaccines. These medicines, distributed through a mix of private and public programs, have greatly reduced the threat of many diseases in the United States over the past century. Two diseases that struck terror in the hearts of American families for generations—smallpox and polio—have been completely eradicated from U.S. shores. Another deadly disease, diphtheria, has been virtually extinguished. Nine other diseases that can be prevented by childhood vaccinations are on the run as well. By 2007, in fact, U.S. rates of hospitalization or death for all nine diseases had fallen by 90 percent or more from their historic highs. Many other parts of the world have made progress in combating these same infectious diseases.

Public health experts and doctors say, though, that the battle against infectious disease is far from over. They emphasize that to fully eradicate other diseases the same way we have eradicated smallpox, we need to further expand immunization programs in the developing world. Another important factor in eliminating these diseases, they say, is to further shore up the safety of water and food supplies in the developing world. Finally, they urge all countries—including the United States—to continue to emphasize the importance of childhood immunization schedules and other defenses that scientists have developed against infectious disease.

CHAPTER 4

Are You Fully Immunized?

In October 2009 thirteen-year-old Timmy Raymond came home from school complaining that he did not feel well. At first his family, who lived in a northeastern Pennsylvania town called Warrington, assumed that he had the same ordinary flu bug that his whole family had been fighting. In reality, though, Timmy and his older brother and parents had all contracted the H1N1 virus, also known as swine flu. This is a highly contagious form of influenza that in some cases can cause severe illness or even death.

The other members of Timmy's family recovered from their bouts with H1N1, but Timmy's condition quickly worsened. Within forty-eight hours he was on life support in a Philadelphia hospital, unable to breathe on his own. Shocked by his swift deterioration, doctors ordered tests that revealed that Timmy's body was not responding to medicines that would have normally helped him fight off the H1N1 virus. It turned out that he also had MRSA (methicillin-resistant staphylococcus aureus), a bacterial infection that is highly resistant to antibiotics.

The combination of the two infections proved too much for Timmy's immune system to overcome. His lung function continued to decline, despite the best efforts of his doctors and the boy's steady bravery. Meanwhile, the Pennsylvania county in which he lived carried out its scheduled H1N1 virus vaccination campaign. It vaccinated seventy thousand people from November 2009 to January 2010.

If Timmy had received one of those vaccinations before encountering the H1N1 virus, he never would have fallen victim to the disease. Unfortunately for him, though, the disease joined with his MRSA condition to assault his lungs. Doctors made desperate attempts to restore his weakened body, but to no avail. "The final effort, a lung transplant,

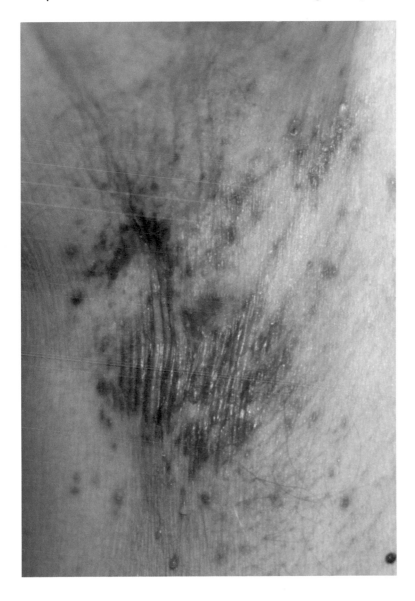

A MRSA skin infection is shown here. MRSA is a bacterium that is highly resistant to antibiotics.

made excruciatingly more complicated because his lungs had dissolved into 'mush' and attached to his chest cavity, proved more than he could withstand," wrote journalist Freda R. Savana. "Although he lived through the 12-hour surgery, he died a short time later."[35] Timmy's death triggered an outpouring of sympathy to his family from the Warrington community. Many friends of the family remembered the boy for his warmth and fun-loving personality. As one of Timmy's coaches said, "He was one of the nicest kids you could ever meet."[36]

The Importance of Seasonal Flu Shots

Timmy Raymond's tragic story is unusual in some respects. Most people who contract the H1N1 virus, for example, do not even require hospitalization. Many people do not even realize they have that particular strain of influenza. They just endure a week or so of chills, headaches, fever, muscle aches, vomiting, and other flu symptoms, then return to work or school when they feel better. The H1N1 flu strain *is* dangerous, however. According to the Centers for Disease Control and Prevention, the 2009 outbreak of H1N1 that claimed Timmy's life was responsible for about 12,500 deaths nationwide. Other types of seasonal flu, meanwhile, can account for 20,000 to 40,000 deaths each year. Most of these flu casualties are small children or senior citizens. All told, the CDC estimates that 13 percent of the U.S. population gets the flu in an average year, and that in some particularly bad years, as many as one out of five Americans contracts some strain of flu.

Little wonder, then, that family doctors and public health experts emphasize the importance of yearly flu shots. Since flu viruses change from year to year, vaccines also are updated to provide protection against the most recent flu strains. "A yearly influenza vaccine is the first and most important step an individual can take in protecting against the flu,"[37] confirmed Jeff Dimond of the CDC. These immunizations not only protect individuals and families from nights of misery and sleeplessness,

FOOD FACT

In most years in the United States, influenza season does not peak until February and ends in April.

Estimated Influenza Vaccination Coverage by Age Groups

Age	Percentage
6 months–17 yrs	51.0%
18+ yrs	40.5%
18–64 yrs	34.8%
18–64 yrs*	46.7%
18–49 yrs	30.5%
18–49 yrs*	39.0%
50–64 yrs	44.5%
65+ yrs	66.6%

*Selected high-risk conditions. Includes people with asthma, diabetes or heart disease.

Taken from: Centers for Disease Control and Prevention. www.cdc.gov/flu/professionals/vaccination/coverage _1011estimates.htm.

they also help keep our nation's economy strong. A survey by the Walgreen's drugstore chain released in late 2011, for example, found that the 2010–2011 flu season resulted in 100 million lost workdays, $7 billion in lost wages, and 32 million missed school days.[38]

Government health care experts and physicians note that flu viruses change over time. In most years, however, scientists are able to adjust flu vaccines so that they immunize people against the viruses circulating at that time. In 2009, for example, Americans looking for protection from ordinary flu as well as the H1N1 strain had to take two different shots. In 2010 and 2011, however, vaccine makers adjusted the product so that their regular flu vaccine also provided immunization against H1N1.

The CDC estimates that about 130 million Americans received flu immunizations for the 2010–2011 flu season. This sounds like a lot, but it actually accounts for only about 41 percent of the total population. Among different age groups, senior citizens did the best job of making sure they got their flu immunizations, with more than 66 percent

People line up for flu shots in Massachusetts. Because flu viruses change from year to year, vaccines are updated against the most recent flu strains.

doing so. The group that performed the worst in this regard was the eighteen to forty-nine age category. Only 30.5 percent of Americans in this age group got their flu shots for the 2010–2011 season.

Flu infections are highly contagious and spread easily in schools, households, churches, child care settings, and workplaces. They can also take a particularly heavy toll on youngsters and adolescents. With this in mind, doctors and public health experts have emphasized the importance of flu immunization to parents.

The American Academy of Pediatrics (AAP) notes that children younger than six months of age are too young to receive influenza vaccine. Everyone aged six months or older, though, should get vaccinated as soon as vaccine becomes available in their community. It takes about two weeks after vaccination for a body's immune system to develop the antibodies that provide protection against flu virus.

Vaccines and Preventable Diseases

In addition to flu vaccines, many vaccines have been developed over the years to ward off infectious diseases. American physicians, pediatricians, and public health experts recommend that healthy infants and children take all ten of these vaccines, which protect against fourteen diseases. "There's a notion out there that all the vaccinations we give to children just seems like too much," admits prominent pediatrician and vaccine researcher Paul Offit. He insists, however, that

> it's not too much. When you're in the womb, you're in a sterile environment. When you enter the birth canal and are born, you're no longer in a sterile environment. Very quickly you have bacteria living on your skin, in your nose and throat. There are trillions of them that live on the surface of your body. . . . So you're constantly handling this barrage of environmental challenges, specifically in the form of fungi and bacteria that live on your body. One bacterium has 2,000 to 6,000 proteins. If you take all fourteen vaccines that kids get, it's probably 150 immunological components or proteins. It's not just figuratively a drop in the ocean of what you manage every day. It's literally a drop in the ocean.[39]

Following are the ten childhood vaccines that are commonly recommended by public health experts and the pediatric community:

DTaP vaccine protects against diphtheria, tetanus, and pertussis (also known as whooping cough) in a single shot. The vaccine needs to be given a total of five times for full immunity. The recommended schedule for these shots for children is at the ages of 2 months, 4 months, 6 months, 15 to 18 months, and 4 to 6 years (before the child enters school). In addition, scientists have developed related vaccines for older patients. Td vaccine is a tetanus-diphtheria vaccine given to adolescents and adults as a booster shot every 10 years, or after an exposure to tetanus under some

Exemptions from Vaccination

Every state requires that children be vaccinated against certain diseases before they can go to school. However, individual states also have established a variety of vaccination exemptions. All fifty states permit exemptions for certain medical reasons. For example, children who are allergic to a vaccine are often excused from taking it. Most states also permit exemptions based on religious objections to vaccination.

Finally, a handful of states have passed laws that allow families to decline vaccination based on philosophical or "personal belief" objections to the practice. However, some states have stipulated that these exemptions cannot be approved until the anti-vaccination parents have met with a health care provider to discuss the benefits and risks of vaccination.

circumstances. Tdap vaccine, meanwhile, also provides extended protection against pertussis. Doctors recommend a single dose of Tdap for adolescents in the 11 to 18 age range and adults in the 19 to 64 age range.

MMR vaccine protects against measles, mumps, and rubella (better known as German measles) in a single shot. The vaccine needs to be given twice for full protection. Doctors recommend that children receive this vaccine at 12 to 15 months old, and then again at 4 to 6 years of age (before entering school).

Varicella vaccine protects against chicken pox. The vaccine needs to be given twice for full protection. Doctors recommend that children receive this vaccine at 12 to 15 months old, and then again at 4 to 6 years of age (before entering school). Recently, however, scientists have developed a single MMRV vaccine that combines the MMR and varicella treatments. Children who get the MMRV vaccine only have to get one shot instead of the two necessary if they take the separate MMR and varicella vaccines, but recipients of the MMRV vaccine are at slightly greater risk of developing a post-immunization fever or other temporary side effects.

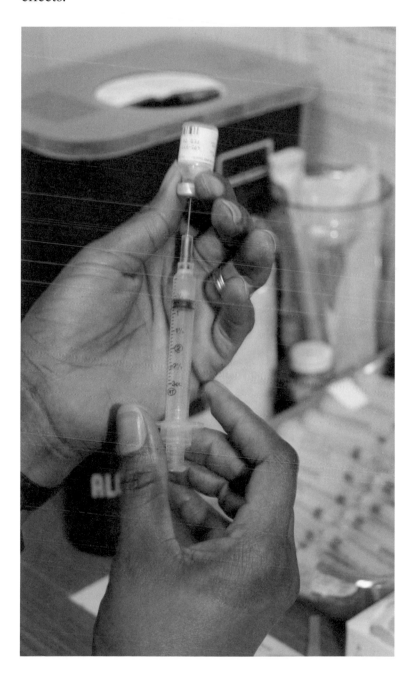

A nurse prepares a dose of DTaP vaccine, which protects against diphtheria, tetanus, and pertussis. The vaccine needs to be given five times for full immunity.

HepA vaccine protects against Hepatitis A. Approved for children who are at least 2 years old, it requires two doses that should be given at least six months apart.

HepB vaccine protects against Hepatitis B. Unlike other vaccines, the first dose of HepB is given at birth. Two subsequent doses are usually given at 1 month and 6 months of age for full immunization. A two-dose version of this vaccine is also available for teenagers who do not get this immunization as infants.

Hib vaccine provides immunization against *Haemophilus influenzae* type b (Hib) bacteria. The recommended childhood vaccination schedule for Hib is at 2 months, 4 months, 6 months, and 15 months of age. There is one brand of Hib vaccine, however, that does not require the 6-month shot.

The seasonal influenza vaccine is recommended for everyone over 6 months of age. Vaccine makers have developed three versions of the flu shot: one for people 6 months to 18 years old, one for adults from 18 to 64 years of age, and one for seniors who are 65 and up.

PCV13 vaccine protects recipients against pneumococcal disease. The standard PCV13 vaccination schedule calls for four doses to be given to infants at 2 months, 4 months, 6 months, and 12 to 15 months. If vaccination is not given or completed during these early months of life, a single-dose version is also available for 2- to 4-year-old kids.

Polio vaccine immunizes children against the poliomyelitis (polio) virus. The United States has used inactivated polio vaccine (IPV) since 2000, but many other parts of the world still use oral polio vaccine (OPV). Doctors recommend four doses of IPV for children, at 2 months, 4 months, 6 to 18 months, and 4 to 6 years old.

Rotavirus vaccine protects immunized patients from the effects of rotavirus, which is the leading cause of severe diarrhea and vomiting illness among children around the world. Two types of rotavirus vaccine are currently recommended by American pediatricians and public health experts for infants. The first vaccine calls for doses at 2 and 4 months of age, while the second vaccine type calls for a third dose at 6 months of age.

One Family's Ordeal with Rotavirus

Brooke Matthys will never forget the week when her two youngest children—her two-year-old daughter and eight-month-old son—were hospitalized with severe cases of rotavirus, an infectious disease that causes vomiting, diarrhea, and dehydration. She will also never forget her feelings of guilt when she heard the diagnosis, because she had put off getting both children immunized for rotavirus. "I now had two children suffering because of me," she said.

Both children eventually recovered, but not before Brooke and her husband spent four sleepless days and nights at the hospital, where the kids were being treated five rooms apart. "[My husband and I] would meet occasionally in the hallway to trade rooms and get updates," she recalled. "It was a long and stressful ordeal that I would not wish on any child or parent. The worst part was that it was totally preventable. If I had taken the time to have my children immunized against rotavirus, this could have all been avoided. Watching your children suffer is awful, but knowing that you could have prevented it, is much worse."

Brooke Matthys. "Two Children Hospitalized with Rotavirus." Immunization Action Coalition, December 29, 2009. www.immunize.org/reports/meningococcus.asp.

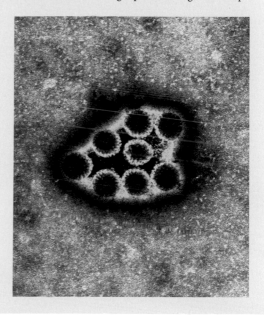

A colored electromicrograph of rotavirus particles, a common cause of intestinal infections in young children.

Many of these childhood vaccines can be delivered to patients at the same office visit. Doctors note, however, that vaccination guidelines vary for children and adults who have other health issues. All of these vaccinations are delivered by shot with the exception of the rotavirus vaccine, which is given orally. In addition, one type of influenza vaccine has been designed so that it can be sprayed up the nose.

HPV and Other Vaccines

One vaccine that has been developed for pre-teen boys and girls has become the focus of a good deal of debate in recent years. The human papillomavirus (HPV) vaccine protects against cervical cancer. This is a form of cancer that starts in the cervix, which is in the lower part of a girl's or woman's uterus. The vaccine protects against this cancer by immunizing patients against human papillomavirus, an infectious disease that is transmitted by sexual activity and is responsible for virtually all cases of cervical cancer. HPV, in fact, is the most common sexually transmitted disease in the country. Approximately 20 million Americans are currently infected with HPV, according to the CDC, which also estimates that

Cervarix prevents infection from certain strains of human papillomavirus that are associated with the development of cervical cancer.

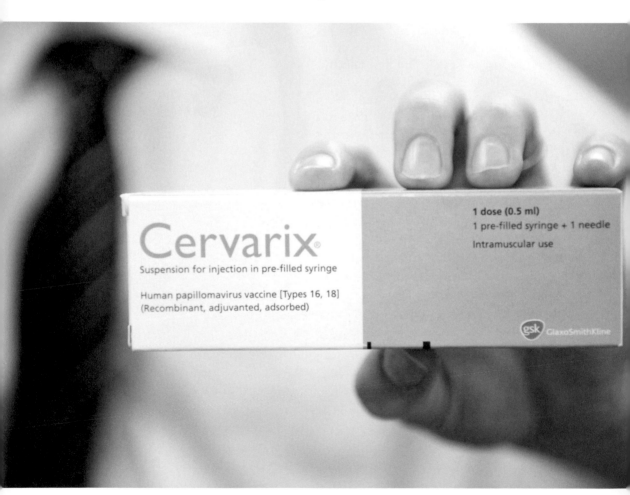

at least half of all sexually active men and women will get it at some point in their lives.

In about nine out of ten cases, people who contract HPV get rid of the disease naturally within two years, usually without developing any symptoms or health problems from it. The risk of getting cervical cancer from HPV is significant for women, though. The CDC estimates that about twelve thousand women a year get cervical cancer, and in nearly all cases their cancer comes from HPV infection. In addition, HPV infections can cause genital warts and rare cancers of the vulva, vagina, penis, anus, mouth, and throat.

In light of these health risks, most pediatricians and public health experts strongly encourage parents to immunize their daughters with the three-dose HPV vaccine at age eleven or twelve. They also encourage boys to get HPV-vaccinated at around the same age. HPV vaccines can also be given to females from ages thirteen to twenty-six, before they are exposed to the virus. Researchers say that these vaccines are safe and can prevent about 70 percent of cervical cancers caused by HPV.

The HPV vaccine has triggered criticism from some conservative parents, lawmakers, and policy analysts, however. They worry that vaccinating girls against a sexually transmitted disease signals acceptance of sexually promiscuous behavior. Most physicians and public health experts—and many parents—disagree with this view. They point out that HPV vaccination is voluntary, and they emphasize that the whole point of the vaccine is to protect their daughters and sons from developing a life-threatening form of cancer in adulthood. In light of the vaccine's clear benefits and proven safety, many supporters have expressed great frustration that

HEALTH FACT

According to a 2011 survey by the Centers for Disease Control and Prevention, nearly one in four teenage girls in the United States mistakenly believes that the HPV vaccine provides protection from a range of sexually transmitted diseases, such as herpes and syphilis. The CDC emphasizes that the HPV vaccine provides protection *only* against human papillomavirus (HPV) infection.

Texas governor Rick Perry met strong opposition to his decision to make all sixth grade girls be vaccinated for HPV.

as of 2010, fewer than four in ten teenage girls in the United States had received the complete three-dose series of the HPV vaccine.

In addition to these immunizations that take place in the offices of pediatricians across the country, scientists have also developed a variety of other vaccines that protect against other diseases. Some of these vaccines are only recommended for certain groups of people. Veterinarians and other people who regularly handle animals, for example, are encouraged to get vaccinated against rabies, which can be passed to humans from diseased animals. Similarly, people who travel to certain areas of Asia, Africa, and Latin America are sometimes encouraged to get immunized against Japanese encephalitis, typhoid fever, and/or yellow fever before they depart.

CHAPTER 5

The Debate over Vaccination and Autism

E ver since the early twentieth century, when vaccination became a standard weapon in America's fight against infectious disease, supporters of immunization have echoed the arguments of Philadelphia physician Jay Frank Schamberg. In 1911 Schamberg wrote:

> When one rides in a railroad or street car, on a ferry-boat or ocean liner, drives in a pleasure vehicle, visits the theater or promenades upon the sidewalk, he takes a definite risk. . . . We read almost daily of deaths from accidents under such circumstances . . . [but] the individual risk is so small as to be generally disregarded. The case is the same with respect to vaccination. When we consider the thousands upon thousands of vaccinations performed throughout the world, and note how rare it is for any death or serious complication to result, we are justified in concluding that the risk attending vaccination in any individual case is practically a negligible quantity.[40]

Over the years, though, opponents of vaccination have argued that Schamberg and his fellow vaccine proponents had it wrong. The anti-vaccination movement has long insisted that the dangers of vaccination have been ignored or

The anti-vaccination movement has long insisted that the dangers of vaccines have been ignored. Protests against the use of mercury in vaccines have happened nationwide.

underappreciated. These concerns are still being expressed today, more than a century after Schamberg made his comments. In fact, the safety and desirability of vaccination have become subjects of particularly fierce debate and controversy in recent years, despite steadfast support for vaccination from the vast majority of American physicians, researchers, and public health experts.

Fears and Criticisms Surrounding Vaccines

Although the human papillomavirus (HPV) vaccine has attracted a lot of attention in recent years, the most heavily publicized debate over vaccination has focused on whether certain vaccines are responsible for incidents of brain damage and rising rates of autism across the United States. Some parents have become convinced that this is the case, and their accusations have received at least some measure of support from a relatively small but sympathetic band of pediatricians, researchers, lawmakers, media personalities, and fellow parents.

The overwhelming majority of pediatricians, scientists, and public health experts who work on vaccination- and infectious disease–related issues insist that there is no basis for these fears. They freely admit that vaccines occasionally cause adverse reactions. They emphasize, however, that studies have found no causal link between vaccination and autism, attention deficit disorder (ADD), or attention deficit hyperactivity disorder (ADHD). Autism is a developmental disorder that severely hinders the acquisition of social and communication skills in children. Both ADD and ADHD are learning disabilities. ADD is a condition in which children have difficulty concentrating. Kids with ADHD have both an inability to focus and an inability to sit still (known as hyperactivity). Finally, proponents of vaccination remind people again and again that vaccines have greatly reduced the threat of illness or death from a host of frightening diseases.

Their assurances have not done much to relieve the concerns of parents who are skeptical of vaccines. In fact, a growing number of parents have decided against immunizing their children with some or all of the vaccines recommended by national health organizations. This trend has angered and frustrated many pediatricians and health care officials, but the anti-vaccine crowd refuses to budge. This deadlock has created all sorts of hard feelings between the two camps. As journalist David Kirby wrote, "Each side accuses the other of being irrational, overzealous, blind to evidence they find inconvenient, and subject to professional, financial, or emotional conflicts of interest that cloud their judgment."[41]

Drawing Connections Between Vaccination and Autism

The first rumblings of concern about a possible link between vaccines and rising rates of autism and other developmental

Vaccinations in the U.S. Armed Forces

Vaccinations are an ordinary fact of life for American men and women who serve in the four branches of the U.S. Armed Forces. Everyone who serves in the Army, Navy, Air Force, or Marines is required to be fully immunized against vaccine-preventable diseases. The U.S. military makes sure that all of its members have all their childhood vaccinations and adult booster shots, and it makes seasonal flu shots mandatory. In addition, military personnel stationed in distant lands are sometimes required to get shots for protection against yellow fever, malaria, and other diseases that pose a public health threat in those regions. Finally, military personnel are sometimes required to undergo vaccination against diseases like anthrax and smallpox at times when the United States believes they could be spread by terrorists or other enemies.

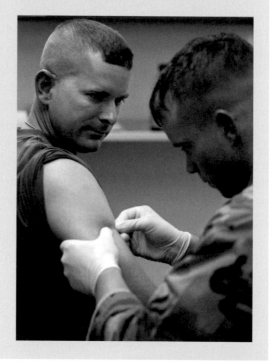

A U.S. Marine receives a smallpox vaccination before being deployed to the Middle East. Every American serviceman and servicewoman is inoculated for many diseases that are a public health threat in the countries they are stationed in.

disabilities were heard in the 1980s. It was not until the late 1990s, though, that these worries began to attract widespread media attention. In 1998 a British researcher named Andrew Wakefield and twelve coauthors printed a study in the British medical journal the *Lancet* alleging that a chemical called thimerosal that was present in the standard single-shot vaccine for measles, mumps, and rubella—the so-called MMR vaccine—might be contributing to rising rates of autism in children.

One year later, the U.S. Public Health Service (PHS), the American Academy of Pediatrics (AAP), and vaccine manufacturers announced their intention to phase out the use of a chemical called thimerosal in all vaccines "as soon as possible." Thimerosol is a preservative that contains trace (extremely tiny) amounts of mercury, a naturally occurring element that can be toxic to humans and other animals at high levels of exposure. At the time of the announcement, thimerosol was a part of a number of important vaccines, including those for diphtheria, tetanus, pertussis, Hib, and hepatitis B.

The AAP and the PHS emphasized that they had found no evidence that the presence of thimerosal had caused any health problems for vaccinated children. To the contrary, they assured Americans that vaccination was very safe and that removing thimerosol was just a sensible precaution. Some

In 1998, British researcher Andrew Wakefield (pictured) and twelve colleagues published a study alleging that the mercury-based preservative thimerosol that is used in vaccines might be contributing to rising rates of autism in children.

parents and pediatricians who had heard about Wakefield's charges, though, were alarmed. In their minds, wrote Kirby, "the government and the AAP were posing an extraordinary contradiction. If thimerosol exposure had been so minimal, and if there was no evidence of harm, then why call for its removal 'as soon as possible'?"[42]

A Growing Movement

By the early 2000s an organized anti-vaccination movement had taken shape. Groups led by concerned parents in Europe, Canada, Australia, the United States, and other parts of the world demanded further testing of vaccines against measles and other diseases to see whether they were responsible for rising rates of autism, ADHD, and other childhood health disorders. Many of these same protesters also claimed that government vaccination requirements violated people's personal freedoms. Some of the most prominent of these anti-vaccine groups in the United States included Talk About Curing Autism (TACA), Generation Rescue, and the National Vaccine Information Center (NVIC).

The anti-vaccine movement has spread its message through traditional media channels like book publishing and television. Much of its growth and influence, however, has been due to its effective use of the Internet. Numerous anti-vaccination websites emerged during the 2000s, and their warnings struck a chord with a lot of parents. "In this new world," observed the PBS news program *Frontline*, "many parents are no longer willing to take the word of their doctor on faith, or to accept the conclusions of the medical establishment."[43]

To anti-vaccination activists, these websites are an invaluable resource. They say that the information contained on these sites exposes the deceitful and unethical behavior of the U.S. government and the health care industry on the issue of vaccination. They also claim

HEALTH FACT

The Centers for Disease Control and Prevention's schedule of childhood vaccines begins at birth and recommends seven different vaccines be given by the time a child reaches six months old.

When Doctors Dismiss Parents

A 2011 survey of pediatricians in nine midwestern states found that a growing number of doctors have become so frustrated with parents who refuse to allow their children to be vaccinated that they have told them to find another doctor for their family health care needs. According to the survey, 21 percent of family doctors have refused to see patients because of the parents' stance on child vaccinations.

Pediatrician Thomas Tyron, who works at Children's Mercy Hospital in Kansas City, Missouri, helped carry out the survey. Tyron says that he now asks parents who want to refuse vaccines or change recommended immunization schedules to find another doctor. He says that he was convinced to take a strong stand on vaccines when a family he was seeing refused to vaccinate either of their two young children. Both then came down with severe cases of pertussis, which can be prevented by vaccination. "In an eighteen-month-old, pertussis is a bad disease," Tyron said. "In a six-week-old, it could be fatal." According to Tyron, the parents' refusal to vaccinate not only endangered their children but could have exposed unvaccinated infants in his waiting room to the disease.

Quoted in Anita Manning. "Refuse Immunizations, Risk Dismissal by Doctor." *USA Today,* November 15, 2011, p. 5D.

that their websites give people the information they need to make an informed choice about vaccinating their children.

Physicians, disease experts, and public health officials, though, believe that these websites do more harm than good. "I think the Internet has been the fuel on the fire of anti-vaccine fears," said Arthur Caplan, who serves as director of the Center for Bioethics at the University of Pennsylvania. "There's plenty of Web sites out there putting out information about people alleging all kinds of complications and problems with vaccines, their own pet theories about what might be dangerous about vaccines, so there are oodles of sources of lousy, dangerous information out there."[44]

People who oppose current vaccination practices have also made extensive use of public hearings to spread their message. These appearances before lawmakers often feature dramatic and emotional testimony from parents who genuinely believe that vaccinations are the source of their child's autism or other developmental disability.

HEALTH FACT

More than 90 percent of unvaccinated people who are exposed to measles contract the disease.

In 2005, for example, activist Elizabeth Birt appeared before a special health committee of the Illinois General Assembly to tell lawmakers about her son. According to Birt, her son was a happy and healthy little boy until he received two vaccinations—an MMR vaccine and a Hib vaccine that contained thimerosol. From that point forward, her son's health declined rapidly and he stopped interacting with the world around him. "We waited and watched and hoped," she recalled. "My son's condition only worsened. He started screaming uncontrollably and rubbing his stomach. It was like watching a fire die out ember by ember and there was no professional who could tell me how my child who had been so full of life and interactive was now in a world of his own."[45]

Despite such accounts, some members of the movement insist that they are not necessarily interested in eliminating vaccines. "Please understand that we are not an antivaccine group," said Generation Rescue president Jenny McCarthy, a celebrity who has become one of America's best-known critics of vaccination. "We are demanding safe vaccines. We want to reduce the schedule and reduce the toxins. If you ask a parent of an autistic child if they want the measles or the autism, we will stand in line for the . . . measles."[46]

Defending the Safety and Necessity of Vaccines

Family doctors, public health experts, and other supporters of vaccination have worked mightily to reassure parents that vaccines are safe. They freely acknowledge that kids who get vaccinations occasionally have mild reactions to the shots, such as redness at the site of the injection or a slight fever. They also agree that in rare instances, kids experience allergic reactions to shots because of the presence of an ingredient that turns out to be an allergen. Vaccination supporters emphasize, though, that numerous scientific studies have

found vaccines to be safe. These studies have found no evidence that vaccines cause autism, ADHD, sudden infant death syndrome (SIDS), or any other childhood health problem that has been blamed on vaccination.

Vaccination advocates also point out that Andrew Wakefield's research, which became the cornerstone of the whole "vaccines cause autism" argument, has come under intense criticism since its release in 1998. In 2004 it was revealed Wakefield's paper featured patients who had been recruited by a lawyer who was already involved in a lawsuit against

Generation Rescue president Jenny McCarthy attends a "shoe dazzle" benefit to raise funds for her safe vaccines campaign.

Andrew Wakefield, center, and associates were accused of serious professional misconduct in their study of children and vaccines. Wakefield was banned from practicing medicine in Britain, and his report was retracted.

vaccine manufacturers. Wakefield was also accused of falsifying his data to provide a link between autism and vaccines. Ten of Wakefield's twelve coauthors eventually withdrew their support for the paper. In 2010 Britain's General Medical Council ruled that Wakefield had engaged in misconduct during the course of conducting and publishing the study. Wakefield was banned from practicing medicine in Britain, and the *Lancet* formally retracted (withdrew support for) its 1998 publication of his paper.

Supporters of vaccination claim that even as new scientific studies confirm the safety of various vaccines, opponents refuse to admit they were wrong. Instead, they constantly shift their hypotheses (claims) about the dangers of vaccination so that the controversy can never be put to rest. Vaccine supporters like Paul Offit describe this strategy as "moving the goal posts." This is a metaphor for when a person who is losing an argument decides to change what the argument is about. "The first hypothesis, which, you know, people bought into long and hard, is that the combination measles, mumps, rubella or MMR vaccine cause autism," states Offit.

> Twelve epidemiological [health] studies showed that that wasn't true. Then the hypothesis shifted to thimerosal, an ethylmercury-containing preservative that was in vaccines, that's no longer in vaccines except for some multi-dose preparations of flu vaccine, that that caused autism. And that clearly has been shown not to be true. So now this is classic [strategy] for pseudoscience, is you just keep moving the goal posts. So now the goal post is, "No, we didn't mean . . . MMR caused autism or thimerosal caused autism, we just meant vaccines in general caused autism."[47]

Defenders of vaccination acknowledge that autism and other developmental disorders are being diagnosed more frequently today, but they argue that this does not mean that vaccines are the cause. They assert that these vaccines simply happen to be delivered at around the same time that autism, sudden infant death syndrome (SIDS), and other childhood diseases and disorders usually appear. "Just because one event followed another, it doesn't mean it was caused by the other," argues Offit. "I mean, every morning, the rooster crows, the sun comes up. It doesn't mean the rooster's causing the sun to come up."[48]

The last argument that pediatricians, scientists, and public health officials level at the anti-vaccination movement is that if immunization rates fall too far in the United States, diseases that have been mostly relegated to the history books could rise again. "Remember, even though many vaccine-preventable illnesses now occur in extremely low numbers, the germs that cause them are still around us, particularly in

In response to the recent outbreak of whooping cough in California, the CDC published flyers in several languages to encourage the public to be vaccinated.

other parts of the world that are as close as a jet plane ride away,"[49] declares the AAP.

In fact, some vaccine-preventable diseases like pertussis (whooping cough) have already become more visible in recent years. In the winter of 2010–2011, for example, California experienced its worst outbreak of pertussis in a half-century. The editors of the magazine *Scientific American* placed the blame for these and other recent disease out-

In response to the recent outbreak of whooping cough in California, the CDC published flyers in several languages to encourage the public to be vaccinated.

breaks squarely on the shoulders of parents who refuse to vaccinate their children. "When immunization rates drop below the critical level [of 95 percent for highly contagious infections like pertussis and measles], disease can strike not only unvaccinated individuals but also vaccinated ones, because all vaccines fail to confer immunity in a certain percentage of people," they wrote. "Parents who opt out [of vaccination] are endangering not only their own kids but everybody else's too—including those who cannot be vaccinated because they are too young or immunocompromised [have a compromised immune system]."[50]

Introduction: A Shield Against Sickness

1. "A History of Vaccines." PATH, April 2009. www.path.org/files/VAC_vacc_history_fs.pdf.

Chapter 1: The History of Vaccination

2. Arthur Allen. *Vaccine: The Controversial Story of Medicine's Greatest Lifesaver.* New York: W.W. Norton, 2007, p. 28.
3. Allen. *Vaccine,* p. 31–33.
4. John Adams. *The Autobiography of John Adams.* Adams Family Papers: An Electronic Archive. Part 1, 1764-1765, sheet 9 of 53. http://www.masshist.org/digitaladams/aea/cfm/doc.cfm?id=A1_9.
5. Elizabeth Anne Fenn. *Pox Americana: The Great Smallpox Epidemic of 1775-82.* New York: Macmillan, 2001, p. 134.
6. Quoted in Allen. *Vaccine,* p. 45.
7. Quoted in "1800: Waterhouse Brings Vaccination to the States." In History of Vaccines Timeline: All Topics. *The History of Vaccines: A Project of the College of Physicians of Philadelphia.* http://www.historyofvaccines.org/content/timelines/all.
8. Quoted in William Howitt. *The History of the Supernatural in all Ages and Nations and in all Churches Christian and Pagan.* Philadelphia: J.B. Lippincott, 1863, p. 241.
9. Genevieve Miller, ed. *Letters of Edward Jenner.* Baltimore: Johns Hopkins University Press, 1983, p. 38.
10. Allen. *Vaccine,* p. 60.
11. Quoted in Allen. *Vaccine,* p. 73.
12. Quoted in Gina Kolata. *Flu.* New York: Farrar, Straus and Giroux, 1999, p. 47.
13. Kevin Hillstrom. *U.S. Health Politics and Policy: A Documentary History.* Washington, DC: CQ Press, 2011, p. 214.
14. Michael Willrich. *Pox: An American History.* New York: Penguin, 2011, p. 338.
15. Quoted in Allen. *Vaccine,* p. 136.
16. James Colgrove. *State of Immunity: The Politics of Vaccination in Twentieth-Century America.* Berkeley: University of California Press, 2006, pp. 69–70.
17. Allen. *Vaccine,* p. 118.
18. Quoted in Allen. *Vaccine,* p. 131.
19. Colgrove. *State of Immunity,* p. 117.

20. "About Jonas Salk." Salk Institute for Biological Studies. http://salk.edu/about/jonas_salk.html.

21. Quoted in Victoria Sherrow. *Makers of Modern Science: Jonas Salk.* New York: Facts On File, 1993, p. 110.

22. PATH. "A History of Vaccines."

Chapter 2: Types of Vaccine

23. American Academy of Pediatrics. "How Do Vaccines Work?" Healthychildren.org, May 31, 2011. www.healthychildren.org/English /safety-prevention/immunizations /pages/How-do-Vaccines-Work .aspx.

24. Centers for Disease Control and Prevention. "How Vaccines Prevent Disease." www.cdc.gov/vaccines /vac-gen/howvpd.htm.

25. Centers for Disease Control and Prevention. "How Vaccines Prevent Disease."

26. National Institute of Allergy and Infectious Diseases. "Vaccines." www.niaid.nih.gov/topics/vac cines/understanding/pages/types vaccines.aspx.

27. National Institute of Allergy and Infections Diseases. "Vaccines."

28. National Institute of Allergy and Infectious Diseases. "Vaccines."

29. The History of Vaccines. "Different Types of Vaccines." www.histo ryofvaccines.org/content/articles /different-types-vaccines.

30. National Institute of Allergy and Infectious Diseases. "Vaccines."

31. Paul Offit. "Vaccinations Battling Disease; People Battling Vaccines." *New York Times,* March 28, 2008. www.nytimes.com/ref/health /healthguide/esn-vaccinations -expert.html.

Chapter 3: Waging War Against Disease

32. PKIDS Online: Parents of Kids with Infectious Diseases. "Silence the Sounds of Pertussis: Family Stories, The Romaguera Family." www.pkids.org/diseases/pertussis /silence_the_sounds_of_pertussis /family_stories.html.

33. World Health Organization. "The End of the Line for Some Infectious Diseases?" In *Removing Obstacles to Healthy Development: World Health Organization Report on Infectious Diseases,* 1999. www.who.int/infectious -disease-report/pages/ch6text.html.

34. Centers for Disease Control and Prevention. *Parent's Guide to Childhood Immunizations.* Atlanta, GA: CDC, 2010, p. 13.

Chapter 4: Are You Fully Immunized?

35. Freda R. Savana. "Remembering a Brave Boy." *Doylestown (PA) Intelligencer,* April 4, 2010. Reprinted in Sharing Personal Stories—Influenza, Children's Hospital of Philadelphia. www.chop.edu/service/parents -possessing-accessing-commu nicating-knowledge-about-vac cines/sharing-personal-stories

/sharing-personal-story-influenza .html#brave-boy.

36. Savana. "Remembering a Brave Boy."
37. Quoted in Marie Rosenthal. "Dispell Myths Among Members Who Fail to Get Their Flu Shots." *Managed Healthcare Executive,* November 2011, p. 7.
38. Walgreens. "Americans Miss 100 Million Work Days and Suffer Nearly $7 Billion in Lost Wages During Flu Season, New Walgreens Flu Impact Report Suggests." Walgreens.com, September 21, 2011. news.walgreens.com/article_dis play.cfm?article_id=5467.
39. Offit. "Vaccinations Battling Disease; People Battling Vaccines."

Chapter 5: The Debate over Vaccination and Autism

40. Quoted in Colgrove. *State of Immunity,* p. 8. From Both Sides of the Vaccination Question. Philadelphia: Anti-Vaccination League of America, 1911.
41. David Kirby. *Evidence of Harm: Mercury in Vaccines and the Autism Epidemic, a Medical Controversy.* New York: St. Martin's Press, 2005, p. xiii.
42. Kirby. *Evidence of Harm,* p. 47.
43. Quoted in *Frontline.* "The Vaccine War," 2010. www.pbs.org/wgbh /pages/frontline/vaccines/.
44. Quoted in *Frontline.* "The Vaccine War."
45. Elizabeth Birt. Testimony before Illinois General Assembly, November 17, 2005. www.adventuresin autism.blogspot.com/2005/12/liz -birt-1956-2005.html.
46. Quoted in Jeffrey Kluger. "Jenny McCarthy on Autism and Vaccines," *Time,* April 1, 2009. www. time.com/time/health/article/0,8 599,1888718,00.html#ixzz1ixwavtyQ.
47. Quoted in *Frontline.* "The Vaccine War."
48. Quoted in *Frontline.* "The Vaccine War."
49. Margaret C. Fisher. *Immunizations and Infectious Diseases: An Informed Parent's Guide.* Elk Grove Village, IL: American Academy of Pediatrics, 2005, pp. 23–24.
50. *Scientific American.* "Fear and Its Consequences: Why States Should Get Tough with Vaccinations," February 10, 2011. www.scientific american.com/article.cfm?id=fear -and-consequences.

antibodies: Natural proteins that the immune system produces to fight viruses, bacteria, and other perceived threats to the body.

antigen: A toxin (such as bacteria) that produces an immune response upon being introduced into the body.

autism: A childhood development disorder marked by an inability to acquire social and communication skills.

causation: The act or process of causing an event to happen.

compulsory: Required.

developmental disability: Severe and lifelong mental and/or physical disability that first appears in early childhood.

exemption: To free an individual or organization from an obligation that others must honor or meet.

epidemic: Widespread outbreak of disease across a region, state, or country.

eradicate: Exterminate or destroy.

immune system: A complex of cells, proteins, and organs that work together to defend the body against viruses, bacteria, and other potential health threats.

infectious disease: Contagious diseases that are spread from a particular source; usually from person to person.

inoculate: To introduce a vaccine or other substance into the body or a person or animal for the purpose of giving that person or animal immunity from a specific disease.

pandemic: Outbreak of infectious disease that extends across multiple countries, a continent, or the world.

vaccine: A medicine that is delivered to a human or animal so that it develops immunity against specific diseases.

variolation: An early, primitive form of immunization.

American Academy of Pediatrics (AAP)

141 Northwest Point Boulevard
Elk Grove Village, IL 60007-1098
phone: (847) 434-4000
fax: (847) 434-8000
website: www.aap.org

The AAP is North America's largest organization of pediatricians and other health care professionals who provide services to infants, children, and young adults. The AAP also maintains a special website (healthychildren.org) that provides lots of information on immunizations and infectious diseases.

Centers for Disease Control and Prevention (CDC)

1600 Clifton Rd.
Atlanta, GA 30333
phone: (800) CDC-INFO; (800) 232-4636
website: www.cdc.gov

An agency of the Department of Health and Human Services, the CDC and its scientific researchers provide the federal government's first line of defense against outbreaks of infectious disease. The CDC maintains extensive web pages dedicated to vaccines and immunization programs.

Children's Hospital of Philadelphia (CHOP) Vaccine Education Center

34th Street and Civic Center Boulevard
Philadelphia, PA 19104
phone: (215) 590-1000
website: www.chop.edu/service/vaccine-education-center/

This special center of the renowned Children's Hospital of Philadelphia provides print, audiovisual, and online information on all aspects of vaccination.

Every Child By Two (ECBT)

1233 20th Street NW, Suite 403
Washington DC 20036-2304
phone: (202) 783-7034
fax: (202) 783-7042
website: www.ecbt.org

This pro-vaccination organization is led by Amy Pisani, Betty Bumpers, and former First Lady Rosalynn Carter. Its self-described mission is to protect all children from vaccine-preventable diseases through educational campaigns that raise parental awareness of the "critical need for timely infant immunizations."

Generation Rescue

13636 Ventura Boulevard, #259
Sherman Oaks, CA 91423
phone: (877) 98AUTISM (982-8847)
website: www.generationrescue.org

Generation Rescue is the most prominent of the parents' organizations that have claimed a link between vaccination and autism in children. Founded by Lisa and J.B. Handley in 2004, the organization provides a wide range of guidance and support resources to families who have children with autism.

Immunization Action Coalition (IAC)

1573 Selby Avenue, Suite 234
St. Paul, MN 55104
phone: (651) 647-9009
website: www.immunize.org

The Immunization Action Coalition maintains a variety of websites, publications, handouts, and other materials designed to educate health care professionals and parents about the importance of immunization and the safety and effectiveness of individual vaccines.

Vaccination News

PO Box 111818
Anchorage, AK 99511-1818
website: vaccinationnews.com

Vaccination News is an online site that gathers anti-vaccination news, editorials, and other information from around the United States and the world.

Books

Centers for Disease Control and Prevention (CDC). *Parent's Guide to Childhood Immunizations.* Atlanta, GA: CDC, 2010. This brochure (which is also available online on the CDC website) provides an overview of vaccination practices and the vaccines that have been developed to fight contagious diseases.

Lauren Feder. *The Parents' Concise Guide to Childhood Vaccinations.* Long Island City, NY: Hatherleigh Press, 2007. This overview of child vaccinations, written by a physician who chose not to vaccinate her children, emphasizes natural approaches to strengthening children's immune systems.

Margaret C. Fisher. *Immunizations and Infectious Diseases: An Informed Parent's Guide.* Elk Grove Village, IL: American Academy of Pediatrics, 2005. This manual published by the American Academy of Pediatrics provides straightforward explanations of various infectious diseases and the vaccines that have been developed to combat them. This work places particular emphasis on explaining what the AAP describes as myths about vaccination.

Seth Mnookin. *The Panic Virus: A True Story of Medicine, Science, and Fear.* New York: Simon and Schuster, 2011. This detailed but accessible work of investigative journalism asserts that the anti-vaccination movement is mostly based on overblown parental fears, irresponsible media coverage, distrust of government, and the rise of the Internet.

David Oshinsky. *Polio: An American Story.* New York: Oxford University Press, 2005. An absorbing historical account of the struggle to eradicate polio from the United States, this work pays special attention to the life stories of Franklin D. Roosevelt, Jonas Salk, Albert Sabin, and other people whose lives were intertwined with the disease.

Websites

CMA Foundation Cervical Cancer and HPV Project (thecmafoundation.org/projects/HPV/index.aspx). This website is the online component of a California Medical Association Foundation project founded to educate both patients and clinicians about the link between the human papillomavirus (HPV) and cervical cancer.

Get Vaxed (www.getvaxed.org). This online project of the PKIDs' Vaccine Initiative works to raise awareness of the importance of immunizations for teens and young adults through the use of edgy videos, conversational discussions of various vaccines, and other tools.

Healthy Children (Healthychildren .org). This online offering of the American Academy of Pediatrics (AAP) contains information on all sorts of health and safety issues pertaining to children and teens, including vaccination.

The History of Vaccines (historyofvaccines.org). This online project of the College of Physicians of Philadelphia provides a treasure trove of informative articles, interactive timelines, student activities, and other information about the history of infectious disease and vaccine development.

PATH Vaccine Resource Library (www.path.org/vaccineresources/). This website is maintained by PATH, an international nonprofit organization that seeks to improve the health and vitality of communities around the world. The site gathers a tremendous array of information on immunization and infectious disease from around the world.

The Vaccine War (www.pbs.org/wgbh /pages/frontline/vaccines/). This is an online presentation of the 2010 PBS *Frontline* special "The Vaccine War." It includes interviews with pro- and anti-vaccination activists, a transcript of the television show, additional readings on autism and vaccines, and a teacher's guide.

INDEX

Influenza vaccination, 66–68, 72
  estimated coverage, by age group,
    67
Inoculation
  problems with, 16–17
  smallpox, 13–15

J

Jacobson v. Massachusetts (1905), 23
Jenner, Edward, 18, 19, *19*

L

Lancet (journal), 81, 86
Lockjaw. *See* Tetanus

M

Massachusetts, Jacobson v. (1905), 23
Mather, Cotton, 13, 14–15, *15*
McCarthy, Jenny, 84, *85*
Measles, *38*, 39, 55–56
  percent of unvaccinated people
    contracting, 84
Measles/mumps/rubella (MMR)
  vaccine, 46, 70
Measles/mumps/rubella/varicella
  (MMRV) vaccine, 70–71
Meningococcal vaccine, 42, *43*
Methicillin-resistant staphylococcus
  aureus (MRSA) infections, 64, *65*
MMR (measles/mumps/rubella)
  vaccine, 46, 70
MMRV (measles/mumps/rubella/
  varicella) vaccine, 70–71
Mumps, 56, *56*
Mumps vaccine, 39–40

N

National Foundation for Infantile
  Paralysis, 31
National Foundation for Infectious
  Disease, 57
National Institute of Allergy and
  Infectious Diseases (NIAID), 37,
  39, 41

O

Offit, Paul, 46–47, 69, 87

P

Pasteur, Louis, 20, 21–22
PATH (Program for Appropriate
  Technology in Health), 8–9, 34,
  60–61
Perry, Rick, *76*
Pertussis (whooping cough), 25,
  48–50, 56
Phipps, James, 18
PHS (U.S. Public Health Service),
  23, 80–81
Pneumococcal disease, 57, 59
Polio vaccine, 72
  oral, 33–34, 40
  quest for, 29
Poliomyelitis (polio), 57, 63
  1916 outbreak of, 23–24
  global mass immunization
    campaigns against, 58–59
  number of cases in U.S., trend in,
    31
  paralytic, effects of, 30
Prevnar, 47

Program for Appropriate
Technology in Health (PATH),
8–9, 34, 60–61

R

Rabies vaccine, 25
Raggedy Ann doll, 32
Ramses V (pharaoh), 13
Recombinant subunit vaccines, 41
Rockefeller Foundation, 34
Romaguera, Gabrielle, 49–50
Rotary International, 34
Rotavirus, 39–40, 60–61
Rotavirus vaccine, 39–40, 71
Roux, Émile, 22
Rubella (German measles), 39–40,
60, 61–62

S

Sabin, Albert, 33, 40
Salk, Jonas, 31, 33, 34, 40
Schamberg, Jay Frank, 77
Smallpox
1721 epidemic, 13
decline in epidemics of, 25
eradication of, 8, 48, 63
Smallpox vaccine, 37, 39–40
virus used in, 40
Spanish Flu (1918), 24
Streptococcus pneumoniae, 47
Swine flu (H1N1), 64–66

T

Td (tetanus-diphtheria) vaccine,
69–70

Tetanus (lockjaw), 62
bacterium causing, 62
contamination of smallpox vaccine
with, 23
number of cases/vaccine coverage
worldwide, 61
Thimerosol, 81–82, 84
Toxoid vaccine, 42
Tuberculosis vaccine, 29, 40
Typhoid fever, 25, 26, 76
epidemic in ancient Athens, 11
vaccine for, 41
Typhus, 11, 24, 27

U

United Nations Children's Fund
(UNICEF), 34
U.S. Public Health Service (PHS), 23,
80–81

V

Vaccination(s)
compulsory, 20–22
doctors' response to parents
refusing, 83
drawing connections between
autism and, 79–82
in early 20th century, 22–23,
26–27
exemptions from compulsory, 70
intranasal, 43–45, 45
opposition to, 22
as patriotic duty, 27–29
public acceptance of, 26
safety/necessity of, 84–89
U.S. armed forces receiving, 28,
80, 80

Vaccines
    childhood, recommendations for,
        69–72, 82
    decline in number of
        pharmaceutical companies
        producing, 46–47
    effects of, 36
    innovations in creation of,
        41–43
    live *vs.* killed, 39–41
    new delivery techniques for,
        43–46
    See also specific types
Vaccinia virus, *40*
Varicella (chickenpox), *51,*
    51–52
Varicella vaccine, 46, 70

Variolation, 13
    See also Inoculation

W

Wakefield, Andrew, 80, *81,* 85–86, *86*
Washington, George, 17
WHO (World Health Organization),
    34, 58–59, 62
Whooping cough. *See* Pertussis
World Health Organization (WHO),
    34, 58–59, 62

Y

Yersin, Alexandre, 22

PICTURE CREDITS

Cover: © itsmejust/Shuttertock.com;
© Christine Langer-Pueschel/
Shutterstock.com; © Nomad_Soul/
Shutterstock.com

© Angela Hampton Picture Library/
Alamy, 49

© AP Images/Harry Cabluck, 76

© AP Images/Reed Saxon, 88

© AP Images/Rex Features, 44

© BSIP/Photo Researchers, Inc., 9

© Chris Maddaloni/Roll Call/Getty
Images, 78

© CDC/Photo Researchers, Inc., 37

© ClassicStock/Alamy, 52

© Everett Collection Inc./Alamy, 24, 33

© Eye of Science/Photo Researchers,
Inc., 40

© Gale/Cengage Learning, 31, 54, 55,
61, 67

© Hercules Robinson/Alamy, 56

© INTERFOTO/Alamy, 19

© James Prince/Photo Researchers,
Inc., 58

© Janine Wiedel Photolibrary/Alamy,
51

© Luke MacGregor/Reuters/Landov,
81

© Mario Villafuerte/Getty Images, 71

© Michael Dwyer/Alamy, 68

© Michael Sweerts/The Bridgeman
Art Library/Getty Images, 12

© Michael Tran/FilmMagic/Getty
Images, 85

© Mike Blake/Reuters/Landov, 80

© Mike Miller/Photo Researchers,
Inc., 73

© Myron Davis/Time & Life Pictures/
Getty Images, 28

© Narinder Nanu/AFP/Getty Images,
60

© Norma Jean Gargasz/Alamy, 45

© North Wind Picture Archives/
Alamy, 15, 21

© Peter Macdiarmid/Getty Images, 86

© Dr. P. Marazzi/Photo Researchers,
Inc., 38, 65, 74

© Popperfoto/Getty Images, 30

© Tek Image/Photo Researchers, Inc.,
43

© 3D4Medical/Photo Researchers,
Inc., 62

ABOUT THE AUTHOR

Kevin Hillstrom is an independent scholar who has written extensively on health and environmental issues. His works include *U.S. Health Policy and Politics: A Documentary History* (2011).